1. Mary of Galilee

MARY of GALILEE

VOLUME I: MARY IN THE NEW TESTAMENT

MARY of GALILEE

Volume I
Mary in the New Testament

Bertrand Buby, SM

ALBA·HOUSE · NEW·YORK

SOCIETY OF ST. PAUL, 2187 VICTORY BLVD., STATEN ISLAND, NEW YORK 10314

Library of Congress Cataloging-in-Publication Data

Buby, Bertrand.
    Mary of Galilee: a trilogy of Marian studies: Mary in the New Testament,
    Mary in the Hebrew Scripture, Mary in the Apocrypha and the sub-apostolic
    writers / Bertrand Buby.
        p.   cm.
    Includes bibliographical references.
    Contents: v. 1. The Scripture texts.
    ISBN 0-8189-0692-8
    1. Mary, Blessed Virgin, Saint.   I. Title.
  BT602.B79   1994
  232.91 — dc20   94-10788
                             CIP

Produced and designed in the United States of America by the
Fathers and Brothers of the Society of St. Paul,
2187 Victory Boulevard, Staten Island, New York 10314,
as part of their communications apostolate.

ISBN: 0-8189-0692-8

Printing Information:

Current Printing - first digit   1   2   3   4   5   6   7   8   9   10

Year of Current Printing - first year shown

1994   1995   1996   1997   1998   1999

TABLE OF CONTENTS

Biblical Abbreviations

OLD TESTAMENT

Genesis	Gn	Nehemiah	Ne	Baruch	Ba
Exodus	Ex	Tobit	Tb	Ezekiel	Ezk
Leviticus	Lv	Judith	Jdt	Daniel	Dn
Numbers	Nb	Esther	Est	Hosea	Ho
Deuteronomy	Dt	1 Maccabees	1 M	Joel	Jl
Joshua	Jos	2 Maccabees	2 M	Amos	Am
Judges	Jg	Job	Jb	Obadiah	Ob
Ruth	Rt	Psalms	Ps	Jonah	Jon
1 Samuel	1 S	Proverbs	Pr	Micah	Mi
2 Samuel	2 S	Ecclesiastes	Ec	Nahum	Na
1 Kings	1 K	Song of Songs	Sg	Habakkuk	Hab
2 Kings	2 K	Wisdom	Ws	Zephaniah	Zp
1 Chronicles	1 Ch	Sirach	Si	Haggai	Hg
2 Chronicles	2 Ch	Isaiah	Is	Malachi	Ml
Ezra	Ezr	Jeremiah	Jr	Zechariah	Zc
		Lamentations	Lm		

NEW TESTAMENT

Matthew	Mt	Ephesians	Ep	Hebrews	Heb
Mark	Mk	Philippians	Ph	James	Jm
Luke	Lk	Colossians	Col	1 Peter	1 P
John	Jn	1 Thessalonians	1 Th	2 Peter	2 P
Acts	Ac	2 Thessalonians	2 Th	1 John	1 Jn
Romans	Rm	1 Timothy	1 Tm	2 John	2 Jn
1 Corinthians	1 Cor	2 Timothy	2 Tm	3 John	3 Jn
2 Corinthians	2 Cor	Titus	Tt	Jude	Jude
Galatians	Gal	Philemon	Phm	Revelation	Rv

INTRODUCTION

On May 28, 1991 the Catholic Telecommunications Network of America offered a one hour presentation on Mary the model of contemporary discipleship. This was the fifth such program in a six-part live telecourse entitled "Vatican II Vision 2000: The Teaching Church."[1] One of the participants of the program was Bishop Emil Wcela, auxiliary of the Rockville Center Diocese in New York. Bishop Wcela outlined the history of Marian teaching given at Vatican II in which the role of Mary within the Church as a model believer in her Son Jesus was emphasized. Mary's place is among the People of God rather than removed from them. The bishops had approved by a narrow margin to include the teaching on Mary within the Council's document on the Church, *Lumen Gentium* (A Light for the Nations). Mary was also presented in a scriptural perspective which focused upon the centrality of Jesus Christ. It was this significant chapter on Mary that liberated theologians, exegetes, liturgists, and artists to think about Mary in a renewed way. Since *Lumen Gentium's* ratification on November 21, 1964 a more scripturally based and ecclesial Mariology has developed. Today the study of Mary is again alive and vibrant in the Catholic Tradition. There were several years, perhaps nearly a decade, of silence and a certain "pondering over" of the role of Mary within the Church; now we are faced with new possibilities arising from the scientific study of the Scriptures and from an investigation of the role of Mary in the thought of the sub-apostolic writers as well as apocryphal texts. These new directions can lead to a more balanced and salutary devotion to Mary, venerated in the Church from earliest times.

This present study, a trilogy on Marian writings, aims to fulfill the direction and vision given by the Second Vatican Council both in the guidelines provided by chapter 8 of *Lumen Gentium* and through the Decree on Divine Revelation (*Dei Verbum*) which says, "Sacred theology rests on the written word of God, together with sacred Tradition, as its primary and perpetual foundation. By scrutinizing in the light of faith all truth stored up in the mystery of Christ, theology is most powerfully strengthened and constantly rejuvenated by that word."[2] A more recent letter from the Congregation for Catholic Education (March 25, 1988) reiterates this direction for the study of Mary: "The study of the Sacred Scriptures, therefore, must be the soul of Mariology."[3]

The chapters presented in this trilogy will follow a common format throughout. First, the actual texts to be studied will be presented. They will be put in the context of the evangelist's own purpose and theology, or, if they are from other writings, within their historical and ecclesial context. The commentary will be a synthesis rather than an analysis since the latter has been offered in the excellent work of the exegetes in *Mary in the New Testament*[4] dedicated to this area of biblical study.

Purpose of the Marian Trilogy

The purpose of this Marian synthesis is to present to the reader the earliest texts which the Church has used to develop its tradition and especially its contemporary images of Mary. Texts from the New Testament, from the Hebrew Scriptures, and from the early ecclesial and pastoral writings will be surveyed for their Marian implications as viewed within the Catholic Tradition. The final section of the trilogy will also include a survey of the Apocryphal

Gospels and the Sub-Apostolic Writings. These materials offer a source from which an exaggerated piety toward Mary developed. From this distorted piety a faulted, inaccurate image of Jesus as well as his mother Mary emerged. Such inappropriate curiosity and excess have always been corrected by the truth of the Gospels and by the authentic teaching of the Church regarding Marian devotions. A scriptural appreciation of Mary provided by such sub-apostolic writers as Ignatius of Antioch, Justin Martyr, and Irenaeus gives us a balanced picture of those earlier centuries in which the first portraits of Mary were emerging in literary form.

The primary foundations for any study of Mary are the references to her in the New Testament. The evangelists made use of the writings known as the Hebrew Scriptures in which they reflected upon the meaning of Jesus as the Christ and as Lord. Through citations from these Scriptures they enabled later Church leaders and theologians to think of Mary in relationship to the Prophets and to certain symbols within the Hebrew Scriptures such as "Daughter of Zion."

The texts of the New Testament are focused on the Christ-Event and therefore are almost exclusively Christological. Mary is involved both in the events of the life of Christ and in his words about the events. For this reason her relationship to Christ has been the subject of study for nearly 2000 years. The Christ-Event is seen as the fulfillment of the Hebrew Scriptures by the evangelists and the other writers of the New Testament. This tandem relationship between the First and Second Covenants or the Old and the New Testaments, permits the study of the person of Jesus in the light of the Hebrew Scriptures which provide the mother soil for substantially ninety percent of the New Testament. A relationship between the texts of both Testaments as well as a relationship between the text and the Event of Christ enables Christian believers to develop further reflection on both the person of Christ and his mother, Mary of Nazareth. Schematically, this relationship of the text to the event can be expressed in the following way:

N.T. text (narrative) <------> Christ-Event (as remembered)

— reflection in the light of the Hebrew Scriptures and its events (Creation, Exodus, New-Exodus).
— incorporation by evangelists and Paul into the New Testament through a development and creative use of these texts, events, and symbols in the liturgy, preaching, and teaching of the Church.

Through the Church's understanding and use of the Scriptures, we see they are not simply chronological or historical accounts but involve revelation in words and events which are meant as a witness to God's working among us. These texts of Scripture reflect the events seen in the light of God's saving plan. The text with its human limitations endeavors to render the event present; there is also a concern on the part of the evangelist or the prophet and the community of believers to make present the events of the past lest they be forgotten. This process which is both the work of the human writer and the influence of the divine thus keeps alive a sacred memory in the community.

In the Christian Scriptures there is a new mode of presenting former texts, namely, a kerygmatic or prophetic way. The New Testament conveys the meaning of the event. The Gospel of John expresses this new mode: "I have said these things while still with you; but the Advocate, the Holy Spirit, whom the Father will send in my name, will teach you everything and remind you of all I have said to you" (Jn 14:25-26).

Even though scientific and sophisticated methods are applied to the texts, and even if we fully accept that the texts are divinely inspired, we are not able to capture the totality of salvific events in the history of God's revelation.

Between the event and the written or oral handing down of the text, there is always interaction and tension between the text and the event. For example, in the Book of Exodus the Passover Event is presented in its simplest ancient form through the text, but later Sapiential literature reinterprets and multiplies the plagues.[5] Despite the radical differerces in these texts there is also a continuity which involves the dia ectic between the original event and its formulation in the Torah, Psalms, and Wisdom. It is this totality of both deeds and words whether written or spoken that constitutes biblical revelation. Today's hermeneutics and exegesis are also a part of the ongoing process of discovering the revelation that God has given us both in texts and events. God's word is thus always alive and active (cf. Heb 4:12-13). This process involving our ecclesial reflections, our personal study, and our own faith reflections helps us to understand God's revelation through these sacred texts and events. In our minds there is this constant dialectic between the text and the event, this going back and forth, this remembering. Perhaps this following diagram may help us visualize the process:

EVENT <--------------------------------> TEXT
   | tradition |
   | |

meaning of what   meaning of what
happened = *hermeneutics* <---------> was written = *exegesis*

The text requires skills of philology, grammar, structure, semantics, and the history of the tradition reached through many methods of interpretatior. The event, on the other hand, is seen through faith. Martin Luther expressed the necessity of both in his statement "Faith is to be built upon history."

Deviations become possible when we do not give sufficient consideration to the tension of both the text and the event and the dialectic existing between them. We can lose sight of the continuity implied in biblical revelation and God's saving action among us. This can and has happened when one wants only to consider the text. This can lead to a literal fundamentalism or even to an allegorical interpretation in which all is for one's own instruction. One is separated from the revelatory event in such a study. Other problems arise when only philological or literary considerations take place, for example, only paying attention to form criticism. In this process the event is forgotten. Another problem is relevancy or radical existential interpretation, that is, "the only real meaning I search for is: What does it say for me in my own modern context?" The final problem occurs when we only look back to what has happened which can be explained solely through history. The text then is already preconditioned by the mind set I have received from Church dogmatics or a closed system of beliefs. Here the text remains mute or becomes a vehicle of polemicism.

In the tension and dialectic between the two we look at both history and exegesis. We interpret the text and at the same time have the event present through faith. Textual truth alone is not historical truth. In the Scriptures, truth is also viewed in the order or dimension of salvation history. In a sense, a believing person is interested in seriously exploring Pilate's question, "What is truth?" (Jn 18:38).

Recent Ecclesial Instruction on Mariology (see Appendix)

William Cardinal Baum, the Prefect for the Congregation for Catholic Education, proposes a plan for the study of Mariology in a vigorous scientific and pastoral way. This particular trilogy is inspired by that proposal and seeks to pursue studies in Mariology which are solidly based on the primary sources of the Christian and Hebrew Scriptures, that is, biblical revelation as read, taught, preached, and lived in the ecclesial community of the people of God. Both the recent Synod of Bishops and Pope John Paul II in his Marian encyclical, *Redemptoris Mater,* have given us the ground plan for reading more carefully the four major constitutions of the Second Vatican Council. The Pope has in his Marian encyclical prepared us for understanding what the Council says about the role of the Blessed Virgin Mary, Mother of God, in the mystery of Christ and the Church. Mary is in fact a *datum,* that is, a "given" of Divine Revelation and a "maternal presence" always operative in the life of the Church.[6]

This particular Marian trilogy offers the reader the basis for Marian study and authent c devotion precisely because it is based on the texts of the New Testament, the Hebrew Scriptures and on a survey of the earliest sub-apostolic writings. It sees Mary as a datum of our faith and as a personal presence that has been with the Church from its very beginning. Mariology does not flow from the Apocryphal, but from the two sacred parts of the Bible, the Hebrew Scriptures and Christian Scriptures. The use of the Bible in the Church testifies to a living tradition which venerates the Mother of the Lord. Whenever exaggerations creep into the Church's understanding there is always a corrective and a new direction offered to the believing community.

Chapter VIII of *Lumen Gentium* has already offered the Church the fullest and most authoritative synthesis about the Mother of the Lord ever to be compiled in a Church Council. This compendium on Mary's role in the history of salvation demonstrates the importance of a biblical understanding of Mary and underlines "the importance of the Sacred Scriptures for a presentation of the role of the Mother of the Lord, truly consonant with the revealed Word."[7]

The Marian teaching of the Second Vatican Council is a holistic approach to our knowledge and study of Mary seen in the Scriptures, the early patristic writings, and in the Church's perennial teaching about the Mother of God through preaching (*kerygma*), through evangelization, through the liturgy, through ecumenical outreach, and in the way of aesthetics (art, music, sculpture) or the way of beauty (*via pulchritudinis*). Mary's presence in the Church is not a peripheral presence; rather through her intimate participation in the history of salvation she "in a certain way unites and mirrors within herself the central truths of the faith."[8]

While essentially a biblical trilogy, the present studies are seen within this overall context of *Lumen Gentium* and the two important post-conciliar documents *Marialis Cultus* (the apostolic exhortation of Paul VI) and *Redemptoris Mater* (the Marian encyclical of Pope John Paul II).

Since the Second Vatican Council (1962-1965) there has

been an impressive development of a theology of Mary. Besides the official documents there are also new frontiers of Mariology which have been explored by biblical exegetes. Studies in Luke, Matthew, and John have reinforced the foundations of Mariology and enriched many of the Marian themes.[9] A more realistic and dynamic development has taken place in the systematic studies of the Marian dogmas: the Immaculate Conception, the Divine Maternity, the Assumption, and the perpetual virginity of Mary. A more critical study of the historical circumstances of these dogmas and their definition continues together with a critical biblical exegetical perspective on the Marian texts which were used in the formulation of these dogmas.

In another area, that of piety and devotion to Mary, both historical and cultural studies have led to a balanced teaching about such devotions. The evaluation of such devotions based on scriptural evidence as well as Church teaching has helped the faithful to grow into a more mature and psychologically sound interest in Marian piety and devotion. Since 1967 six International Marian Congresses were organized by the Pontifical International Marian Academy in Rome which systematically studied the manifestations of Marian piety from the first to the twentieth century.

Ecumenical studies have produced numerous books and articles on Mary. John Paul II has emphasized "how profoundly the Catholic Church, the Orthodox Church, and the ancient churches of the East feel united by love and praise of the Theotokos." Mary's title of *Theotokos* means God-bearer. Demetrius I, the ecumenical patriarch, states, "our two sister Churches have maintained throughout the centuries an unextinguished flame of devotion to the most venerated person of the all-holy Mother of God." He added, "The subject of Mariology should occupy a central position in the theological dialogue between our Churches.. for the full establishment of our ecclesial communion."[10]

The Reformation Churches have also been a part of this dialogue. Several Churches have invited Catholic scholars to present ideas about Mary from the Scriptures. Studies on Mary as a woman of faith and as a disciple of the Lord have appeared in the writings of these Protestant scholars. The dialogue offers a good balance: not "obscuring" the person of Mary or the primordial principle of holding on to her as a datum of Revelation.

There have also been presentations about Mary the Jewish mother of Jesus in the Jewish-Christian dialogue. Several such sessions have taken place in Rome in 1986 and in Dayton, Ohio where the first lay-directed group of the Dayton Christian-Jewish Dialogue holds regular monthly meetings. Mary as the "Daughter of Zion" offers a promise of future development for this interchange between Jews and Christians. Mary's own Jewishness helps many Christians to see Judaism as the matrix for their own belief in the person of Jesus and his words in the Gospels.

Other important areas of development are the studies of Mary from an anthropological point of view where she is seen as an archetype of the Mediterranean woman. An entire issue of the *Biblical Theology Bulletin* (Vol. 20, Summer, 1990, No. 2) is dedicated to a study of Mary in which there are challenging statements about her and her image in the Mediterranean atmosphere which surrounds the New Testament. Other studies by Christian feminist theologians and by those in the arts (the *via pulchritudinis*) are also developing in the area of Marian studies.

Finally, the careful and cautious attitude of the Church towards recent Marian apparitions challenges us as believers to be faithful to the Gospel and the sacramental life of the Church.

Such are the many concentric circles of influence and theology surrounding the study of Mary in the present era.

The Conciliar documents and papal statements of Paul VI and John Paul II suggest several working principles which assist both the faithful and the scholars in seeing Mary always in the history of salvation, in her relationship to the supereminence of her Son Jesus Christ, and as a primary model of what the Church is called to be in modern society. (See paragraphs 18, 19, and 21 of the "Letter from the Congregation for Catholic Education.")

These principles and guidelines have been followed carefully in two centers for Marian studies which offer both a licentiate and a doctorate in theology. The centers are mentioned in Cardinal Baum's letter: "This Congregation has been pleased to note the dissertations for the license or doctorate in theology which have treated Mariological themes. Persuaded of the importance of such studies and desiring their increase, in 1979 the Congregation instituted the "license or doctorate in theology with specialization in Mariology" (cf. Ioannes Paulus PP. II, Const. Ap. *Sapientia Christiana* (15 Aprilis 1979) Appendix II ad art. 64 "Ordinationum," n. 12: *AAS* 71 (1979), 520). Two centers offer this specialization: The Pontifical "Marianum" Faculty of Theology in Rome, and the International Marian Research Institute, University of Dayton, Ohio, U.S.A., which is linked to the Marianum" ("Letter," paragraph 31, footnote 59).

Cardinal Baum's letter appears in the Appendix since it was the incentive for this trilogy. I am also indebted to the following persons for their assistance in preparing the text: Patricia Phipps of the International Marian Research Institute, Brother Don Sullivan, S.M., Ron Novotny, Marge Yefchak, Jean Sullivan, and Eileen Moorman — teachers, students, and friends in this endeavor.

We are now ready to begin our study of the texts which are pertinent to a solid foundation for a theology of Mary. These studies are meant to be seen in their Christological and ecclesiological contexts.

The first section begins with the initial foundation for all that follows from the Hebrew Scriptures, the ecclesial writings, and the Apocrypha, namely, the texts on Mary from the New Testament. A chronological approach will enable the reader to see the development of a trajectory of thought and symbol for the person of Mary. These studies will also proceed from a faith context that is confident both in the divinely inspired texts and in the living and authentic Tradition of the Church and in its teaching authority. The work is dedicated to those who have understood and accepted the *Fiat mihi secundum verbum tuum* of Luke 1:38. "Let it be done to me according to your word."

Endnotes

[1] Catholic Telecommunications Network of America, 3211 Fourth St., N.E., Washington, DC 20017-1194. Tel.: (202) 541-3444 FAX: (202) 541-3313.

May 28, 1991: "Vatican II Vision 2000," Part 5 of 6: "Mary: Model of Contemporary Discipleship."

[2] *The Documents of Vatican II*, ed. Walter M. Abbott, S.J., Guild Press, New York, 1966, p. 127 ("Dogmatic Constitution or Divine Revelation," 24).

[3] "Letter from the Congregation for Catholic Education," Rome, 25 March 1988: "The Virgin Mary in Intellectual and Spiritual Formation," paragraph 24. Reprint in *Marian Studies* 39 (1988), The Marian Library, University of Dayton, Dayton, Ohio 45469-1390, p. 216.

[4] Brown, R. E., et al. (eds.), *Mary in the New Testament: A Collaborative Assessment by Protestant and Roman Catholic Scholars* (Philadelphia: Fortress; Ramsey, New Jersey: Paulist, 1978).

[5] Compare Exodus 7:8-13:16 with Psalms 78:43-51; 105:26-36; and Wisdom 11:5-19:22.

[6] "Letter from the Congregation for Catholic Education," *Marian Studies* 39, p. 204, #1.

[7] "Letter," p. 205, #4.

[8] "Letter," p. 208, #5.

[9] "Letter," p. 206, #6.

[10] "Letter," p. 211, #14.

MARY of GALILEE

VOLUME I: MARY IN THE NEW TESTAMENT

Chapter One

PAULINE FORESHADOWING
OF A JEWISH WOMAN

The Texts

1. Galatians 1:19; 4:4-5; 4:28-29 written around 54-55 C.E.

"I did not meet any other apostles except *James*, the *Brother* of the Lord . . ."

". . . but when the designated time had come, God sent forth his Son *born of a woman*, born under the Law, to deliver from the Law those who were subjected to it, so that we might receive our status as adopted sons . . ."

"You, my brothers, are children of the promise, as Isaac was. But just as in those days the son born in nature's course persecuted the one whose birth was in the realm of the spirit, so do we find it now."

2. 2 Corinthians 5:14c-17 written in autumn of 57 C.E.

". . . since one died for all, all died. He died for all so that those who live might live no longer for themselves but for him who for their sakes died and was raised up."

"Because of this we no longer look on anyone in terms of mere human judgment. If at one time we so regarded Christ, we no longer know him by this standard. This

means that if anyone is in Christ, he is a new creation. The
old order has passed away; now all is new."

3. Romans 1:3-4; 9:4-5 written near 58 C.E.

". . . the gospel concerning his Son, who was descended
from David according to the flesh but was made Son of
God in power according to the spirit of holiness, by his
resurrection from the dead: Jesus Christ our Lord."

". . . the Israelites. Theirs were the adoption, the glory, the
covenants, the lawgiving, the worship, and the promises;
theirs were the patriarchs, and from them came the Messiah
(I speak of his human origins). Blessed forever be God who
is over all! Amen."

4. Philippians 2:6-8 written around 61-63 C.E.

"Though he was in the form of God, he did not deem
equality with God something to be grasped at. Rather, he
emptied himself and took the form of a slave, being born in
the likeness of men. He was known to be of human estate,
and it was thus that he humbled himself, obediently accepting even death, death on a cross!"

Chronologically, the Pauline writings are the first Scriptures
of the New Testament in its written form. Paul writes most of these
letters between 51 C.E. and 63 C.E. His letters do not treat of Jesus'
words and deeds as do the later Gospels, but rather concentrate on
the Paschal Mysteries of Christ seen as his redemptive action upon
all humanity through his death and glorious Resurrection. Paul's
writings spring from his singular experience of conversion through
the Risen Christ's intervention in his own life. We can see then that
he has little to say about the historical aspects of Jesus' life, hence,
any recollection he may offer to us concerning those who surrounded Jesus is going to be minimal. We can understand why he
is so succinct and parsimonious when it comes to recalling the
woman who was the mother of Jesus. As we will see, she is only

implicitly remembered by Paul in a most indirect way in Galatians 4:4. The other lines in Paul which are selected for our Marian study and reflection speak more of the human condition of Jesus, his Davidic heritage, and his being born into the laws and prescriptions of Judaism.

Before looking more closely into the Marian foreshadowing in the Pauline writings, the following portrait of Paul will give us a helpful background to understand the commentary offered on the texts with remote Marian implications.

Paul is thoroughly Jewish and is proud of his heritage as a Jew. In Galatians he gives us his personal testimony of this in saying, "You have heard, I know, of the story of my former way of life in Judaism. You know that I went to extremes in persecuting the church of God and tried to destroy it. I made progress in Jewish observance far beyond most of my contemporaries, in my excess of zeal to live out all the traditions of my ancestors" (Gal 1:13-14). In Philippians he continues along the same lines: "If anyone thinks he has a right to put his trust in external evidence, all the more can I! I was circumcised on the eighth day, being of the stock of Israel and the tribe of Benjamin, a Hebrew of Hebrew origins; in legal observance I was a Pharisee, and so zealous that I persecuted the church. I was above reproach when it came to justice based on the Law" (Ph 3:4-6). Paul will continue to share this Jewish heritage in his epistles and personal letters addressed to the early Christian communities. He is contemporaneous with the emerging of Christianity throughout the contours of the Mediterranean and as an itinerant preacher and teacher he testifies to his own religious convictions and belief in Jesus Christ as Messiah and Risen Lord. His gospel is really the preaching about Jesus and his salvific death through Resurrection. His presentation of the Christian gospel is authentic (1 Cor 15:1-4), radical (1 Cor 1:18-25), personal (Ph, chapters 1 and 2), spirit-filled (Rm 8), and apostolically commissioned by God (seen especially in the introductions of each epistle).

The central theme of all the Pauline writings is Jesus Christ. In fact, his Christocentrism is so strong that the expression "in Christ" (*en Christo*) appears 154 times. His preaching of the good news or gospel of Jesus Christ parallels his centering on Christ as the Redeemer or Savior (*Soter*, cf. 1 Cor 2:1-5). This positive thrust is present in all of the Pauline literature in which God predestines, calls, justifies, and glorifies all men and women who believe. It becomes evident that the Christocentrism of Paul represents an emerging Christianity which becomes more and more Hellenistic. The Lordship of Jesus, the pre-existence of the Son, and the beginnings of Trinitarian expressions like the distinction of God as Father, Jesus as Son, and the Spirit are spread throughout the Pauline epistles. Though we might be able to make a rough theological classification or synthesis of Paul, the experience of Paul through the reading of his letters leads us to see Paul as a person who is deeply concerned with the Person of Jesus not only in himself but also in all believers and the believing communities or the churches to whom Paul ministers. His description of Baptism (Rm 6) and the Eucharist (1 Cor 11) involve the believer and the believing community.

Paul is abundantly rich as a person because of the many-faceted dimensions of his background. His Pharisaic training and commitment come through most of his writings in his manner of argumentation, his symbolism, and his belief in the resurrection of the body. He has fully lived and accepted the prophetic message of the Hebrew Scriptures which he cherished and knew by heart (let us remember that he relied on the Septuagint to reach the Gentiles and the Jews of the Diaspora). He boasts of the tradition and heritage of his Jewishness (Gal 1 and 2, Ph 3). Hellenism also has a profound influence on him for we see his knowledge and use of the Koine Greek, his interest in city and civic life, Greek poetry and culture, sporting events such as boxing and running, and Greek philosophy and religion. His writings are a fascinating study of how to use and change the values of a pagan culture without destroying its external beauty and form. His personal experience of the Risen Lord results in the most profound conversion to Christianity (*metanoia*) that history has ever attested. Paul becomes all things to all men and women because of Christ. For Paul to live is Christ and his message is to make others become more and more aware of their possible union with Christ whether they be Jew or Gentile. Paul is faithful to the tradition of the early Christian preachers, but he is creative and energetic in bringing his universalism to all of the Christian communities as a special apostle called by God.

Paul's underlying *parenesis* (encouragement) for all who come in contact with him is bound up in triads of words or virtues: faith or trust (*pistis*), hope (*elpis*), and love (*agape*); joy, peace, and confidence — especially in the conclusions of his letters. Both the introduction, the thanksgiving, and the conclusions of his writings encourage the Christians to develop these triads within their lives and to live in the optimism of the victory of Christ over sin and death. Paul encourages them to become who they really are in Christ. This is but one of the existential and progressive ideas in Paul which are inspirational for the believing Christians.

Paul is one of those rare persons who is intuitive, passionate, brilliant, and exacting at the same time. His later letters show us how much of a sensitive and concerned person he is for the sake of others. Despite some of his harsh language, Paul is very fond of and committed to his friends in Judaism and Christianity. He makes no distinctions between men and women friends though he does contrast their roles and submits to some of the inequities stressed by the society of his time. There are some areas of religious and cultural concerns where the Body of Christ can grow beyond Paul's adherence to his culture: for example, his emphasis on the contrast of the Law over against the Love of Christ, his eschatological expectancy of an immediate return of Christ, and his concern for conversion of the Jewish People. Womanhood can be seen in the light of modern Christian values rather than Paul's cultural presuppositions. Slavery is in no way to be condoned as it was even in Paul's writings. We can sum up Paul's message as: "So faith, hope, and love abide, these three; but the greatest of these is love" (1 Cor 13:13).

The Selected Texts of a Pauline
Foreshadowing of a Jewish Woman

In Paul's letter to the Galatians the three references used in this study are Galatians 1:19; 4:4-5; 4:28-29. This epistle was probably written at Ephesus around 54 C.E. Paul is preparing for his final apostolic mission of itinerant preaching and teaching to the newly formed Christian communities. How appropriate that later Christian tradition will see Ephesus as a great Marian center where the Mother of Jesus is said to have lived out her life with the Beloved Disciple! In 431 C.E. the Council of Ephesus would adopt officially the title of *Theotokos* or God-bearer for the Mother of Jesus.

In Galatians Paul is trying to keep the Christians faithful to the Gospel that he has preached. He is struggling to wrest them from seeking to fulfill Jewish prescriptions of the Law which are being advocated by a conservative faction within the Galatian churches.

In our first text, Galatians 1:19, we read that Paul consulted the followers of Jesus: "I did not meet any other apostles except James, the brother of the Lord . . ." This James is not to be confused with James son of Zebedee nor with James son of Alphaeus. He is called the "brother" of the Lord (*adelphos tou Kyriou*) and was considered the first overseer (*episcopos*) of Jerusalem (Eusebius, *Ecclesiastical History*, 2.23.1). Since this term in Greek (*adelphos*) primarily can mean blood brother, this text becomes a factor in any considerations about the perpetual virginity of Mary. In both the New Testament and in the Septuagint translation of the Hebrew Scriptures the term brother can mean kinsman in an extended family such as is the custom of calling one a brother in Africa or in the Arab speaking nations today. It can also mean a relative or cousin as attested in Greek papyri. In the most recent Catholic commentary written in the *New Jerome Biblical Commentary*, Joseph Fitzmyer, S.J., says "Mary, the mother of James the Little and Joses" can scarcely be used by the evangelist to designate the mother of the person crucified on Calvary; *adelphos*, used of James, is best understood as "kinsman, relative." In reading different commentaries on this text one will discover that the interpretation normally takes on the position with regard to Mary's virginity that is held or not held by the religious persuasion to which the interpreter belongs. Catholics, Roman and Orthodox, therefore, do not understand the text as referring to another son of Mary, the mother of Jesus. The discussion of this topic will be taken up more fully in Chapter Two of this book, in our consideration of Mark's Gospel where there is a mention of "Mary, the mother of James the Little and Joses" who is not the same Mary as the mother of Jesus. Let us remember that Mary was a very commonly used name and that at the foot of the cross in John's Gospel there are possibly four women called by the name of Mary! In Mark's Gospel the references are Mark 6:3; 15:40,47; and 16:1.

In the text of Galatians 4:4 Paul gives us his most explicit reference to a Jewish woman giving birth to the Messiah under the Law of Judaism. This is the most important text of Paul for any Marian study or reflection even though it is also very general and indeterminate. Up to about 1800 C.E. the text was understood as an implicit reference to the mother of the Son of God. Since that time, theologians and exegetes have been divided into four groups. They are: (1) Those who pass over the question of Mary's virginity in silence; (2) Those who categorically state that Paul does not speak of a virgin-mother for the Son of God; (3) Those who say that Paul neither says anything about Mary's virginity nor anything against it; and (4) Those who maintain that the virginity of Mary is affirmed by this text.[1]

From an exegetical point of view, the expression "born of a woman" (*genomenon ek gunaikos*) is the most important in our study. There is also a variant found in Galatians 4:4 which reads "to be begotten of a woman" in which the aorist participle is used (*gennomenon* from the verb *gennao* meaning to beget). This latter variant emphasizes the male principle of begetting and is used repeatedly in Matthew 1:1-17. In the first century of the Common Era these two verbs tend to be used similarly, hence the variant reading. In the preferred reading of Galatians 4:4 a second aorist participle is used (from *ginomai*) which expresses the once and for all historical aspect of this birth, hence, the translation "who was born of a woman." The participle likewise shows simultaneity with the principal verb attesting to the coming of the fullness of time.

Albert Vanhoye, S.J., in a masterful study of the structure of this passage demonstrates that the text says, "the Son of God was born of a woman."[2] He thereby states that the divine maternity is affirmed by Galatians 4:4. This is important for Mariology for we can say anachronistically this is Paul's first principle of Mariology. She is the mother of the Messiah who is Son of God. Even so, we are still in the shadows and as Père Lagrange said so well, "The purpose of Paul is not to emphasize the prerogatives of Jesus of Nazareth, but to show the abasement (the kenosis, the humble origins) of the Son of God." Church teaching in the recent encyclical of John Paul II, *Redemptoris Mater*, would affirm this principle of St. Paul. However, there are exegetes who do not see the divinity of Christ implied in this expression and, even less so, a basis for a Mariology.

Structurally there are five elements present in our text after the announcement of the event in salvation history (Paul's continued emphasis on Incarnation-Redemption theology):

A. God sent his Son — (a Divine Action) = the Son is sent
B. Who was born of a woman — (modality) = born of woman
C. born under the Law — (modality) = submits to the Law
D. in order that we might be free from the Law — (finality) = to liberate us from the Law
E. so that we might receive — (finality) = have adoption conferred on us by God[3]

In this structural analysis we see modality in B and C, that is, what Jesus has in common with us in his humanness. There is no emphasis on the privileges such as being born from a virgin. The expression "born of a woman" is present in both the Hebrew and Christian testaments (*yelud isshah* = *gennetos gunaikos*) and is present in Job 14:1, 4; 15:14; 25:4 and Wisdom 7:3; it is also found in the Dead Sea Scrolls as "child of a woman" or "creature of earthly clay" (see I QH 18:12-13 and I QH 13:14-15).

The structure shows a chiastic mode especially seen in C and D in the expression "under the Law." B is related to E in an antithetical way (descent/ascent). A and E are related, for Jesus is seen as Son of God in A. We note also that the Son is sert (Gal 4:4), then the Spirit is sent (Gal 4:6; cf. also Gal 1:1, 10, 12, 16).

According to the structure the text does not affirm the virgin-motherhood of Mary nor does it deny it. It has some of the same elements which appear in the Infancy Narratives of Matthew and Luke wherein Jesus is presented (1) as the Son of God (2) who is born of a Jewish woman (3) without the father Joseph being an active agent in this birth. No mention of a father is made in the Pauline text.

Vanhoye also discusses the importance of the use of paradox in Paul, and for that matter in the rest of the New Testament.[4] By means of a paradoxical understanding of certain texts we can go beyond the structure of the text to its modality. The structure shows the antithetical parallelism of the lines; the expressions used, however, go beyond ant thesis to the modality of paradox. Paul already has used a paradox in Galatians 3:13-14 which is close to our text of Galatians 4:4. A paradox evokes surprise; it then beckons us to reflect more deeply on the meaning of its words. For example, how can Christ be a malefactor of the Law and at the same time a liberator from it? This is the paradox of 2 Corinthians 5:21; Galatians 1:4; 2:20; and 1 Corinthians 1:18-25. The Hebrew Scriptures offer us an even more apparent paradox in Judges 14:8, 14.

In the history of the tradition about the text certain theologians have seen the virginity of Mary within this text precisely because there is no mention of a human father. Cyril of Jerusalem (349-387 C.E.) writes: "God sent forth his Son, made of a woman ..." which means made *only* of a woman, that is, from a virgin (*ek parthenos*). Cyril is reversing the arguments of his opponents as he continues, "for we have already demonstrated that a virgin is also called 'woman'" (*P.G.* 33:755 A, also in Buby, *Biblical Exegesis in Greek Patristic Texts*, p. 238, published in Dayton, 1979).

Theodore of Mopsuestia, a contemporary of Cyril, but living in Greece and working from a more literal-historical method of interpretation likewise says: "Our blessed Fathers omitted all these things and said: *and was born of Mary and crucified in the days of Pontius Pilate*, because the beginning of His economy for us is one thing and its purpose or end another, hence they included both these headings, one right after the other, all those things that the Gospel taught us. He was born of the Virgin Mary as a man, according to the law of human nature, and was made of a woman. Indeed the Apostle said thus: 'God sent forth His Son, made of a woman, made under the Law, to redeem them that were under the Law, that we might receive the adoption of sons.' In saying that he was made of a woman, he showed that he entered the world from a woman . . . Many things, as we have already said, happened to him according to human law; things which we may learn from the Gospel. He was wrapped in swaddling clothes after he was born and was laid in a manger; he was circumcised according to the custom of the Law and was brought to the temple according to the Mosaic Law; he was shown before the Lord enduring all things dealing with his increase in stature, wisdom, and favor, while remaining subject to his parents. He practiced in a right way all things dealing with the justification from the Law; he then received baptism, from which he gave the New Testament as in a symbol; he endured the temptation of Satan and bore upon himself the toil of journeys and the offering of prayers with great fervor; and, so as to shorten my sermon, he performed all the work of the Gospel with much labor and sweat, showed much patience with his enemies, and finally drew nigh unto death by crucifixion, through which he abolished death by his resurrection from the dead" (*Theodore of Mopsuestia*, Woodstock Studies, Vol. V, p. 67 by A. Mingana).

　　We can see that Theodore may have implicitly seen in the text of Galatians 4:4 a reference to Mary as the only parent of Jesus. There may have been an earlier tradition from which both Cyril and Theodore drew. John Chrysostom, another contemporary, uses the text of Galatians 4:4 with the accommodated use of Baruch 3:38 in his second homily for the Feast of the Nativity of Christ (Christmas was just beginning to be celebrated as a feast at this time) to show the reality of Christ's human nature and the effectiveness of the redemption (*Ecloga*, hom 34. PG 63:823 D). Theodore also in his commentary on Galatians speaks of "the human nature of Jesus Christ, as *Son from the line of David* or Son of the woman Mary who is the object of divine benevolence" (*Commentarium in Epistolam ad Galatias*, Swete, I, p. 62). Theodore makes these declarations of faith based on the text of Galatians 4:4 and on the phrase from the Nicene Creed which he is explaining to those preparing for Baptism. Once again, this is not strict historical exegesis of the text, but an ecclesial interpretation that helped the faithful to understand the human origins of Jesus. Another text of Theodore that is close to Galatians 4:4 is the following: "In this way we should also think about Christ our Lord. It was a novel thing to have been fashioned from a woman without marital intercourse, by the power of the Holy Spirit, but he is associated with human nature by the fact that he is from the nature of Mary and it is for this that he is also said to be of the seed of David and Abraham, as in his nature he is related to them" (A. Mingana, op. cit., p. 67).

Paul, therefore, sets the stage through Galatians 4:4 for the Jewishness of Jesus through the woman from whom he is born into salvation history at the appointed time God has chosen. We will come to see that the Pauline texts about the human origins of Jesus are quite rich and valuable for explaining the Jewishness of Jesus and his Messiahship. This early Christian *Kenosis*-Christology which emphasizes the limitations and humble status of Jesus is to be balanced with the exaltation of Jesus through the power of God in the Resurrection. Paul will affirm that the importance of knowing Jesus according to the flesh is now no longer of prime importance for him, but it was necessary to state these human limitations of his being born into Judaism and under the umbrage and prescriptions of the Law. In these all too succinct statements of Paul there are historical foundations which attest to the reality of Jesus in history because he was born of a woman of Jewish origins. Paul does not mention her name because he always is focusing on Jesus Christ.

As a digression, it is interesting to listen to and to read what

Jewish scholars and teachers write and say when they are asked to speak about the mother of Jesus the Jew. Usually, they choose reflections taken from the heroines of Judaism like Ruth, Esther, and Judith. From them they paint a portrait of a Jewish woman typical of the biblical culture before the time of Christ. In 1986 at an International Symposium on Mary held at the Marianum in Rome, Avital Wohlmann, a Jewish scholar, spoke of "Why the Silence of Judaism Today on the Subject of Mary of Nazareth?"[5] She spoke from an existentialist and philosophical point of view and empha- sized that Mary is really of no interest to the modern Jew. She was, however, challenged by the Dominican scholar Marcel Dubois, O.P., who as an Israeli citizen said that he experienced Mary's presence in the Jewish women on the streets of Jerusalem. His insistence was on the covenant begun with Moses and carried through not as a contradiction but as a continuity in Christianity. He also developed a sketch of Mary from the Hebrew Scriptures through the title "Daughter of Zion." We will return to this in the second part of our trilogy. Some further Jewish reflections can be gathered from Geza Vermes' book on Jesus the Jew, in which he flatly denies any of the Christian beliefs about Mary. More positive are the few but fortuitous insights of David Flusser where he sees Christians coming to an understanding of the Holocaust through the sufferings of the woman who was the mother of Jesus.[6] Such observations coming from Jewish scholars are important for us in learning how to see the historical Mary within her proper setting as a Jewish woman of the first century. We also should be aware that most of these studies would be applicable to any woman of the first century. The specificity of Mary of Nazareth, however, consists in her unique relationship to Jesus of Nazareth, the Messiah for the Christian world. Paul, of course, saw Jesus as a continuation of all that had been said and promised by God about the Messiah of Judaism.

In the excellent ecumenical study, *Mary in the New Testament*, edited by R. E. Brown there is a chapter on Paul which proceeds from the method used in this book on all of the references used from the

New Testament to speak of Mary.[7] This work establishes a rigorous and near exclusive use of the historical-critical method. There is also an ecumenical concern to reach a type of consensus on the understanding of the Marian texts which are studied. There is a strict chronological approach which separates later interpretations of the Patristic period from primitive Christianity. The book is an excellent resource tool for the study of this particular trilogy which takes in a more ecclesial and Catholic approach while respecting the excellent scholarship offered by the editor and authors of *Mary in the New Testament*. In the above-mentioned study, Father Joseph Fitzmyer, S.J., developed and led the discussions that resulted in the chapter on Paul. He offers an excellent analysis of the key words used in Galatians 4:4 and affirms that they are definitely directed to a Christology and not a Mariology.[8] It is through his human birth that Mary as woman is all important for Jesus the Messiah. Such Greek words from the text like *genomenon* from *ginesthai* (to be born of), *kata sarka* (according to human flesh) which is contrasted with *kata pneuma hagiosynes* (according to the spirit of holiness) (Rm 1:4) *ek spermatos David* (from the seed of David), *Christos* (Messiah or Anointed One), *en dunamei* (by the power of), *gennan* (to be begotten) *horsithentos* (appointed or designated), *huiou theou* (of the son of God) *ton adelphon tou Kyriou* (the brother of the Lord in Gal 1:19), *genomenon ek gunaikos* (born of a woman) become a source for deepening our understanding of the human nature of the Messiah born of a Jewish woman.

The reader is encouraged to consult modern commentaries on the passages presented here and to look carefully at the words which treat of the human origins of the birth of the Messiah and his eschatological extension as Christ the Lord through his resurrection according to the power of God's Spirit.

Pauline symbolism is always to be seen and enlivened through its matrix which is Biblical Judaism. It is Paul who presents Christ, the Messiah, as the New Adam of the new creation. Christ is also the first fruits of the Resurrection. Paul sows the seeds for the concept of the New Eve in such references to Christ as the New Adam. The Johannine communities would expand this symbol to Mary as the "woman" of the new creation theme; this is one step closer to the concept and development of Mary as the New Eve. Justin Martyr and Irenaeus make the direct connection in this symbolism with Mary. The parallelism between the two is still being studied in conjunction with the important correctives and observations made by feminist exegetes concerning a negative absolutizing of Eve. It becomes an important symbol for the ecclesio-typical aspect of Mary. Most of the important developments started with Irenaeus, a defender of women in the second century. Justin, Clement of Rome, and Tertullian are among the early writers who also have noted such a parallelism.

Galatians 4:4 in Tertullian

In concluding this section on the most important passage that Paul uses for a Marian reflection, the following texts should show how the reference to Mary was used in the earliest centuries of the Church.

Tertullian who lived from 155/160 C.E. to 240/250 C.E. wrote a treatise called "The Veiling of Virgins" (6, 1) about 206 or 213 C.E.:

"Writing to the Galatians (the Apostle) says: 'God sent his own Son, born of a woman' (Gal 4:4), who certainly is admitted to have been a virgin, even if Ebionites deny it. I acknowledge, too, that the Angel Gabriel was sent to a virgin (Lk 1:26-27). But when he blesses her, he ranks her not among virgins but among women: 'Blessed art thou among women' (Lk 1:28). The angel knew that even a virgin may be a woman (Gal 4:4). Certainly there is nothing here that may be regarded as having been spoken prophetically, as if by saying 'born of a woman' the Apostle was naming her as one who was about to become a woman, that is, married; for he was not able to name her as formerly a woman, of whom Christ was not to be born, that is, one who had known man. But she who was present, she who was a virgin, was called a woman in consequence of the meaning of the word applied in the widest sense to a virgin as included in the universal class of women."

This passage has been understood by some to speak against the virginity of Mary. To others it seems quite the opposite. Tertullian seems to be saying that Mary is called a virgin at the time of the Annunciation as given by Luke. Paul refers to her as a woman in the fact that Jesus the Christ is born of her. Paul cannot thereby mean that she was not a virgin at the time of Christ's birth. For if Mary, a virgin at the time of the Annunciation, was not to be still a virgin at the time of Christ's birth, Paul would not have called attention to it, because it would have in no way been remarkable. That a woman who bears a child is a virgin is worth noting; that she is not a virgin requires no notice. Nor could she have formerly known man, for she is called a virgin at the Annunciation. So when Paul calls her woman, whatever he means, he is not thereby distinguishing woman from virgin. Tertullian concludes she is called woman merely as a generic term, and a virgin more specifically. In the present passage, then, so far from denying her virginity, Tertullian is proved to have believed in the virginity *ante partum*, while saying nothing whatever of virginity *in partu* and *post partum*. These two he does deny in another writing.

Galatians 4:28-29

Paul frequently uses an allegorical approach in interpreting passages from the Hebrew Scriptures. Our text is of interest for it speaks of our spiritual adoption as children of God who are free-born just as Isaac was born according to God's promise and not according to the flesh. Sarah, Isaac's mother, represents those who are free because of her faith. Isaac, the promised child, is a symbol for Jesus, while Hagar represents those bound to the limits of the Law and her son Ishmael is a slave-born son under the prescriptions of the Law. Paul knows the Mosaic Law has not yet been promulgated, but in his allegorizing the historical events are suspended.

Time stands still and all is seen at once. Paul has developed this allegorical interpretation at some length (Gal 4:21-31). Isaac and then Jesus are the "sons of the one born free" (Gal 4:30). Isaac is considered to be a "child born according to the Spirit" (Gal 4:29) because of Sarah's and Abraham's faith. Jesus, too, as we learn from Matthew and Luke is a child born through the operative action of the Holy Spirit in the believing virgin of Nazareth, Mary. Does Paul imply that Isaac was conceived through the activity of the Spirit without a human father as agent? According to the early Palestinian tradition of rabbinic Judaism, it is God who helps Sarah and Abraham to have a son (cf. Gn 21:1-14). Paul who is allegorizing could have been influenced by Philo (25 B.C.E. - 41 C.E.) and Hellenistic Judaism which records this interpretation about Sarah's conception: "The Lord visited Sarah as he had said, and the Lord did to Sarah as he had promised." This, or an interpretation similar to this, could have influenced Paul as he allegorized the passage in Genesis which he uses to compare with our own adoption as children of God.

In these texts of Paul from Galatians, we can say that the Apostle does not sow the seeds of Mariology, but through his choice of words and ideas about the birth of the Messiah, the soil in which the seed is to be sown is carefully cultivated and displayed. More recently, John Paul II, in the very beginning of his Marian encyclical, *Redemptoris Mater*, cites Galatians 4:4 because he finds an empowering theological concept of salvation history in Paul's "fullness of time"; moreover, he discovers that the mother of God's Son is united with him in Judaism and in his salvific mission (cf. J.M. Hennaux, S.J., *N.R. Th.* Jan.-Fev., 89, p. 29).

2 Corinthians 5:14c-17

Why did I choose this text which does not have anything to do with Mary? I think this text helps us to learn why Paul does not present Jesus to the churches in the same genre as the Gospels. Paul's experience of Jesus is that of the Resurrected Christ, not the palpable Jesus of the Gospels. He never knew or saw Jesus personally as did Mary Magdalene, Peter, James, John, and Martha. Paul's experience of Jesus is totally bound up with the Paschal Mysteries and their redemptive effects upon all peoples. His is a totally faith-oriented experience in Christ. This text, therefore, helps us to understand why there are not many words of Jesus in the Pauline writings (except 1 Cor 11:23-25). Mary, of course, is not even mentioned for she too belongs to this historical and physical dimension of being with Christ. Paul is predictable. His great emphasis is on Redemptive Christology. His Christology is thoroughly soteriological in its expression.

The *New Jerome Biblical Commentary* interprets verse 16 in this way: "'We judge no one in a fleshly way': As a Pharisee, Paul had judged falsely because of his uncritical acceptance of current Jewish opinion. 'We know him no longer': There must be in a similar way a radical shift in the way believers assess other human beings" (50:25, p. 822).

Romans 1:3-4; 9:4-5

These are among the final lines that Paul wrote probably around 58 C.E. They are important for understanding the Jewishness of Jesus and the gifts of grace and nature which he inherited from Judaism. Paul, as is his custom, addresses the believing community of Rome and leads his readers into the themes of the epistle through an early tradition that he had received about the Messiah. His own gospel about Jesus Christ is always faithful to what he received both from a revelation from God and from the apostles themselves whom he had consulted after his conversion. He sees the divine plan being fulfilled both through the revelation given to Judaism through its leaders and prophets, and, of course, in its Sacred Writings. Jesus Christ who is born into Judaism is the Revealer par excellence for him and for the Christian communities which he was to found, nourish, and teach. The contrasts between what Jesus receives from nature as a Jew, and from grace through the Spirit of holiness, are presented in the brief kerygmatic or creedal statement he shares with the believers in Rome through verses 3 and 4. Jesus is said to be descended from David according to the flesh, therefore, Jesus belongs to the royal messianic line (for that matter so did hundreds of others who were contemporaneous with him). Jesus also, however, according to the Spirit of holiness is empowered as the Resurrected Son of God. Both sketches of the human and the divine are present in Christ; the former leads to the latter and they are mutually within the same person. Grace always builds on nature.

Romans 1:3-4 is the earliest reference to Jesus as the promised Messiah born into the family of David. An outline would present what Paul is contrasting in the kerygmatic statement as follows: Humanness: "the Messiah was born" (modality = through a Jewish mother). He was born "from the seed of David" (we will learn of the importance of Joseph, the foster-father of Jesus, through Matthew's first chapter). "According to the flesh" = a further description of the modality, that is, he is born of Mary. Divine likeness: Jesus was made or designated Son of God in power according to the Spirit of holiness through the resurrection from the dead.

Scholars understand the above statements as having their provenance from the earlier kerygma which was used to explain who Jesus is to the believers of the early Church. This probably was already being proclaimed in the forties of the Common Era. Paul makes use of this creedal expression in his introduction to express the relationship by human descent or kinship in the Davidic-Messianic line. Paul, unlike later New Testament writers, is not interested in the manner of Jesus' birth nor who his parents were. These are interests of a generation of Christians who would follow after Paul. The Infancy Narratives of Matthew and Luke would take up such questions.

In chapter nine of Romans Paul returns to the human ancestry and heritage of Christ: "To them (Paul's Jewish brothers and sisters) belong the patriarchs, and *of their race according to the flesh, is the Messiah* (the Christ). God, who is over all, be blessed forever" (Rm 9:5). Again Paul is only interested in the Messiah, not his parents. We will, however, come to know more about these relationships in the Gospels some twenty years later. Then the Davidic lineage will be explained in greater detail (the sign of a later tradition) and the names of Joseph and Mary will be given (also the sign of a later tradition; cf. Matthew 1:16-17; 1:18-25). These connections through Judaism and its royal ancestors become important factors in the belief of Christians about Jesus Christ as the Messiah born of the Virgin Mary.

In summarizing what we have said about the passages chosen thus far, we can say that several Catholic scholars see an indication of Mary's virginity in the fact that Paul uses the verb *ginesthai* in Romans 1:3, Philippians 2:7; Galatians 4:4. They assert that had Paul wanted to stress the fact that Jesus was born of a human father he would have used another verb which clearly means to be begotten by a human father, namely, *gennasthai*. Father J. Fitzmyer, however, has a better interpretation in seeing the text of Romans 1:3-4 as a reference more to the Resurrection than to the manner of his human birth:

"Paul's real goal in the parallelism of Rm 1:3-4 is not so much to connect Jesus with the Davidic line as to affirm that Jesus, the Davidic Messiah, is risen. To read more into the use of the verb *ginesthai* in Rm 1:3 (or for that matter in Galatians 4:4 or in Philippians 2:7) is over-interpretation and is close to eisegesis" (*Mary in the New Testament*, p. 38).

Thus in this pre-Pauline formula Jesus is designated Son of God in power through the Resurrection. Such a statement is the beginning of a trajectory of thought resulting in later Christian formulations about the human and divine natures in Christ, especially in the Councils of Nicea in 325 C.E. and at Ephesus in 431 C.E. The contrast of the phrase that Paul presents shows us that Jesus "according to the flesh" is related to humanity through the Davidic lineage, whereas Jesus "as designated according to the Spirit" is related to God who raises him from the dead. Unlike Luke,

Paul never uses "Spirit" to refer to the active power of God in the conception of Jesus (cf. Lk 1:32, 35; Mt 1:20). In Luke it is from the action of the Spirit that the virginity of Mary is rendered fruitful.

Philippians 2:6-8

Our final biblical reflection about Jesus in relationship to Mary of Nazareth is taken from the earliest Christological Hymn that we have. It is found in Philippians 2:5-11 and was written between 57-63 C.E. Paul borrows this hymn from the Jewish-Christian community and uses it for his cherished Philippian believers. P. Grelot suggests that the hymn may have originally been written and sung in Aramaic (*Biblica* 54 [1973], pp. 176-186).

The hymn shows Jesus as not clinging to his divine status. Rather he empties himself (his *kenosis*) as a servant or slave (*doulos*) by taking on our human nature. The hymn contains two humiliations of Jesus balanced by a twofold exaltation as the hymn comes to a close in verses 10 and 11. There happens to be a remarkable similarity in its meaning and in several of its words to the hymn attributed to Mary called the Magnificat (Lk 1:46-55). Precisely in the lowliness of Christ (*tapeinoun*) and in his servant quality (*doulos*) there is a parallel to Mary's considering herself the handmaid (*doule*) of the Lord because God has looked upon her lowliness (*tapenosis*).

There is indication of a descending-ascending pattern in the Christology of the hymn in the contrast offered by verse 6 and then followed by the rest of the strophes. Verse 6 reads: "Who, though his condition was divine, did not consider being like to God something to exploit for selfish gain . . ." And, in verse 9: "Wherefore God has highly exalted him and graciously bestowed upon him the name that is above every other name." This seems remarkably close to the pattern in the hymn of John's Prologue (Jn 1:1, 11, 14, 18). There are also resonances of this hymn in John 17:5 and Hebrews 1:3. Some exegetes speak of the pre-existence of the Word of God in these lines of Philippians and their parallels. Such a Christology can be schematized in this way:

Pre-existence of *the Word* at God's side

descent among us

exaltation

This pattern differs from the Christology of the Synoptics which is described more as linear, with an ascending-exaltation of Christ at his death and Resurrection but not containing the notion of the pre-existence of Jesus as Word:

born of Mary ——— *Son of God*

Is it possible that such an early hymn could have contained such a high Christology while emanating from an early Palestinian Christian milieu? Scholars are divided on the question. Yet, it is such passages read and sung in the churches that led to more precise Trinitarian formulations in the third and fourth centuries. Moreover, the hymn may have even been the one Pliny the Younger mentions to Trajan in his letter touching upon the worship of the Christians who "sing a hymn to the Christ as to a god" (*Epistola* 10:96, circa 111-113 C.E.).

I conclude that some of the most profound and exalted statements about Jesus flow from the hymn and its use in liturgical celebrations. Verses 7 and 8 then could be considered as having a Christological-Marian implication:

"But rather he emptied himself (*ekenosen*)/ adopting the condition of a slave (*doulos*)/ taking on the likeness of human beings./ And being found in human form he lowered himself (*etapenosen*) further still/ becoming obedient unto death (even to death upon a cross)."

A Marian implication may be seen in the above verse where the "emptying out" and the "being born or being found in human form" are referred to in the person of Jesus, the Christ. The word for birth (*ginesthai*) and the word for servant (*doulos*) are the echo of a Marian implication here. If we recall Paul's words at the opening of this hymn: "Have this mind among yourselves, which you have in Christ Jesus," the encouragement means that this person who now is God-man has totally emptied himself in becoming human and has taken on the nature of a servant or a slave by becoming human. Jesus took his human nature from his mother, Mary. Like her who called herself the "handmaid" (*doule*) of the Lord (Lk 1:48), this hymn calls Christ the "servant" (*doulos*). The emptying out of Jesus is complemented by the lowliness, the openness, and the poverty of Mary who totally emptied herself before God to be filled with God's Word. God in the person of Jesus likewise emptied himself to take on the same characteristics of a servant by being born of a Jewish maiden, Mary of Nazareth. These written words, then, offer us a thin trace of the presence of Mary. We also have to recall that there is the tradition that Luke was a companion of Paul. The expression of Philippians 2:7 is evocative of Mary's Magnificat in Luke's Gospel. The characteristics of faithful discipleship are present in both the Christ whom Paul is praising and in Mary who is totally dependent on God. She is one of the poor of Yahweh (*anawim*) who are referred to in the Psalms and who trust so magnanimously in God. Her obedience and humility are other dispositions that are similar to those expressed in the Pauline use of the hymn. In the same verse, the word "being born" (*ginesthai*) can only factually be understood of the woman who brought forth the Christ.

These are the ten or so lines in the entire Pauline Corpus that have been studied and reflected upon in reference to remote connections to Mary. Though we have only a confirmation of her humanness and the Jewish heritage she bequeathed to her Son, these are seminal concepts which are important for the foundation of Paul's Christology. They are, as he has said in Romans, based on the human origins of Jesus and his empowering holiness through

God's raising him from the dead. Mary, his mother, is most assuredly involved in his being one like us. In summary we can say that Paul tells us that a Jewish woman brought Jesus forth into the fullness of God's saving action in history. She did so under the mantle of the Torah.

Endnotes

1. *Theotokos: Ricerche interdisciplinari* (Roma: Montfortane, I, 1993/2). This third issue of the publication of the Italian Mariological Society has 6 articles on Galatians 4:4. There are brief summaries at the end of each entry.

2. A. Vanhoye, S.J., "La Mère du Fils de Dieu selon Ga 4,4," *Marianum* 40 (1978) pp. 237-247.

3. See p. 241.

4. See pp. 244-245.

5. Avital Wohlmann, "Mary of Nazareth: Why the Silence of Judaism?" *SIDIC* 20 (No. 2, 1987) pp. 9-14.

6. J. Pelikan, D. Flusser, J. Lang, *Mery: Images of the Mother of Jesus in Jewish and Christian Perspective* (Philadelphia: Fortress, 1986, pp. 7-16).

7. R.E. Brown, et al (eds.) *Mary in the New Testament* (Philadelphia: Fortress; New York/ Ramsey, N.J.: Paulist, 1978, pp. 33-49) [*MNT*].

8. *MNT*, pp. 41-49.

Chapter Two

MARK: THE FIRST GOSPEL
IMAGE OF MARY (65-70 C.E.)

Mark's Gospel is of supreme importance as a historical document because it is the first writing to be called a Gospel. It is also the foundation and source for the outline and development of Matthew and Luke apart from their Infancy Narratives. The Fourth Gospel (John) has some Marcan resemblances as well. "There are grounds for suspecting Aramaic sources behind the Gospel, though whether written or oral it is impossible to say" (cf. M. Black, *An Aramaic Approach to the Gospels and Acts*, 2 ed., 1954). The importance of this is that a work so deeply colored by Semitic usages must, in the main, bear a historical value (V. Taylor). It has sometimes been alleged that the Gospels derive much of their coloring from the theology of the Hellenistic Church, but in Mark we are very close to the original source in oral (Aramaic) tradition (R. McL. Wilson, in *Peake's Commentary on the Bible*, Thomas Nelson, London, 1964, p. 800).

Beginning in 1870 the excitement about discovering historical facts, words, and deeds of Jesus arose from a newly discovered interest in the vivid and enthusiastic account of Mark's Good News. The proponents of form criticism (1917-1940) kept this excitement at a high pitch as the pursuit of the historical Jesus continued until as recently as fifty years ago. Through careful analytic studies the earliest oral and written traditions were set forth and established Mark as the most primitive and original Gospel. Presently, even though this enthusiasm for discovering the real Jesus of history is less prominent, Mark continues to be a key to Synoptic studies especially regarding Jesus' active ministry, his preaching of the Kingdom, and call to discipleship.

Outside of the New Testament references to a person named Mark or John Mark (Ac 12:12,25; 13:5,13; 15:37-39; 1 P 5:13; Col 4:10; Phm 24, 2 Tm 4:1), the earliest written recollection of the Gospel of Mark comes from a statement made by Papias of Hieropolis (circa 140 C.E.) recorded in the fourth century by Eusebius: "This also the presbyter used to say: 'When Mark became Peter's interpreter, he wrote down accurately, although not in order, all that he remembered of what the Lord had said and done.' For he had not heard or followed the Lord, but later, as I said, (heard and followed) Peter, who used to adapt his teaching to the needs (of the moment), without making any sort of arrangement of the Lord's oracles. Consequently, Mark made no mistake in thus writing down certain things as he remembered them. For he was careful not to omit or falsify anything of what he had heard" (Eusebius, *H.E.*, 3.39; GCS 9/ 1, 290-292).

Mark's theology is centered on Jesus who is the proclaimer, healer, and teacher of the in-breaking of the Kingdom of God. Jesus ushers in the era of salvation by his words and actions, especially by his death on a Cross and the promise of his Resurrection. Mark's Gospel beckons its readers to become disciples. This theology of Mark is consistent throughout its simple geographical outline: (1) Jesus' baptism and announcement of the Kingdom; (2) his active ministry in Galilee; (3) his journey to Jerusalem; (4) his suffering, death, and Resurrection. While reading or studying any part of Mark's Gospel this outline and theological perspective should be envisioned.

Mark's Gospel, then, is the earliest in traditions about Jesus. It has a certain greening vigor about it which may spring from the Galilean surroundings of Jesus. Mark brings us his message in bold, clear, and descriptive patterns. He captures the freshness, newness, and exuberant hope that the Good News of Jesus brings to those who hear it for the first time. It is with such expectation, then, that we also approach this Gospel to discover what it says about Mary, the Mother of Jesus. What type of an image of Mary does Mark give to the reader?

In Mark, as we will discover, we have a clear silhouette of a devout Jewish mother who is concerned about the activity of her son, Jesus. Most of the background for our assertions about her come from the context which surrounds the first scene in which she appears, Mark 3:31-35. Chapter three read in its entirety gives us the proper perspective for Mark's imaging of Mary. We will see that Mary is very vigorous in her efforts to intervene in Jesus' life when it seems to be endangered or when his activity may detract from the reputation of Mary's family.[1]

In contrast to Paul, the Marcan image of Mary is no longer obscure, but more definite, precise, and explicit. Even though Mark has approximately the same number of lines about her, they do say more than Paul has said. To Mark we owe the honor of naming her for us for the first time (Mk 6:3). Here are the two pericopes that are important for this study:

> [31]Then his mother and his brothers came; and standing
> outside, they sent to him and called him.
> [32]A crowd was sitting around him; and they said to him,
> "Your mother and your brothers and sisters are outside
> asking for you."
> [33] And he replied, "Who are my mother and brothers?"
> [34] And looking at those who sat around him, he said, "Here
> are my mother and my brothers!
> [35] Whoever does the will of God is my brother and sister and
> mother." (Mk 3:31-35)

> [1] He left that place and came to his hometown, and his
> disciples followed him.
> [2] On the Sabbath he began to teach in the synagogue, and
> many who heard him were astounded. They said,
> "Where did this man get all this? What is this wisdom

> that has been given to him? What deeds of power are
> being done by his hands!
> ³ Is not this the carpenter, the son of Mary and brother of
> James and Joses and Judas and Simon, and are not his
> sisters here with us?" And they took offense at him.
> ⁴ Then Jesus said to them, "Prophets are not without honor,
> except in their hometown, and among their own kin,
> and in their own house."
> ⁵ And he could do no deed of power there, except that he
> laid his hands on a few sick people and cured them.
> ⁶ And he was amazed at their unbelief (Mk 6:1-6a).

Mark 3:31-35 is our first pericope of interest. It is the source
for parallels in Matthew's Gospel (Mt 12:46-50) and Luke's (Lk
8:19-21). Here is the parallel study:

[Matthew 12:46-50]	[Mark 3:31-35]	[Luke 8:19-21]
⁴⁶ While he was still speaking to the people, behold, his mother and his brothers stood outside, asking to speak to him. [⁴⁷Some one told him, "Your mother and your brothers are standing outside, asking to speak to you."] ⁴⁸But he replied to the man who told him, "Who is my mother, and who are my brothers?" ⁴⁹And stretching out his hand toward his disciples, he said, "Here are my mother and my brothers! ⁵⁰For whoever does the will of my Father in heaven is my brother, and sister, and mother."	³¹And his mother and his brothers came; and standing outside they sent to him and called him. ³²And a crowd was sitting about him; and they said to him, "Your mother and your brothers [and your sisters] are outside, asking for you." ³³And he replied, "Who are my mother and my brothers?" ³⁴And looking around on those who sat about him, he said, "Here are my mother and my brothers! ³⁵Whoever does the will of God is my brother, and sister, and mother."	¹⁹Then his mother and his brothers came to him, but they could not reach him for the crowd. ²⁰And he was told, "Your mother and your brothers are standing outside, desiring to see you." ²¹But he said to them, "My mother and my brothers are those who hear the word of God and do it."

In Mark this selection is a self-contained unit, but in carefully
examining the repetitions and additions, one notices the signs of a
development by the final redactor, Mark. (We will note something
similar in the development of the Cana account in the Fourth

Gospel, Jn 2:1-11.) The style is characteristically Marcan with the use of many "ands" (*kai*) as a connective word and also through the use of the present tense and the present participle. This gives a continuous flavor to the scene and keeps the reader attentive to the intense activity of Jesus so prevalent in this Gospel.

The powerful, succinct saying of Jesus at the end of the pericope is Mark's motivation for recalling this early tradition about the relationship of Jesus to his family. Form critics call this a pronouncement story precisely because it preserves Jesus' words which demonstrate that his true family are those who do the will of God who alone is Father to Jesus in this Gospel. Hence, the saying has an eschatological meaning for the Marcan listener or the Marcan community. Jesus who calls God his Father throughout this Gospel completes the family image by speaking of brother(s), sister(s), and mother. The quality of relationship to God which Jesus expects is an imitation of his own. Mark thus captures this connectedness with Jesus through a spiritual bond between the believer and God. Those who understand and accept this call are truly brother, sister, and mother to Jesus.

Martin Dibelius prefers to see the original saying of Jesus consisting in "Behold, my mother and brethren." The pericope then serves as a paradigm for the believer. Rudolf Bultmann calls it an ideal scene from the earliest recollections about Jesus. Perhaps, Dibelius' observations are better appreciated if we see them in the context of the parallel in Luke 11:27-28: "While he was saying this, a woman in the crowd raised her voice and said to him, 'Blessed is the womb that bore you and the breasts that nursed you!' But he said, 'Blessed rather are those who hear the word of God and obey it.'" As is customary in Judaism Jesus gives a blessing after receiving one. An example of this continues in modern Judaism. Upon entering a home the host says to a guest, *Baruch ha bah!* (Blessed the one arriving), and the guest answers, *Baruch ha nimtsah!* (Blessed the one found here).

Our pericope also fits in well with the overall flow of the story which begins in Mark 3:19b and continues to 3:35. In one of the greatest commentaries on Mark that has been written, Vincent Taylor has this important insight: "It is intended by Mark as a sequel to the earlier story (3:19-30) and serves this purpose excellently, but long before he incorporated it into his Gospel (or the complex 3:19-35) the narrative was current and gained its form in oral tradition. It is a rounded whole from which much has fallen away by a process of attrition determined by an interest in the question of the true kindred of Jesus" (V. Taylor, *The Gospel According to Mark*, St. Martin's Press, London, 1966, p. 245).

Mark 3:19b-3:30 forms the context for our study of the Marian pericope of 3:31-35. In the *New Revised Version* it begins: "Then he went home; [20] and the crowd came together again, so that they could not even eat. [21] When his family heard it, they went out to restrain him for people were saying, 'He has gone out of his mind.'" The vocabulary and style are Marcan; however, the section is now seen as an independent tradition in its own right. There is no parallel for 3:19b-21 in the other Synoptics. Mark has his own theology and tradition about the members of Jesus' family. What follows from this introduction to Jesus' whereabouts is a series of narratives and sayings which illustrate some of the charges that are being brought against Jesus even in this early stage of his ministry. This opposition to Jesus is recorded by Mark; the section can be broken into four parts:

3:19b-21: The fear and concern of Jesus' family
3:22-26: Judgment against Jesus; he is in collusion with Satan
3:27-30: Sayings about the strong man and blasphemy
3:31-35: On the true kindred of Jesus

If we read this entire section and then study the last pericope on the true kindred of Jesus we come to a better understanding of why Mark ends with the scene of Jesus' mother and brothers and sisters.

Mark starts this section by writing quite freely without any indication of a source. The house and the crowd are the focal points. Mark uses the historic present while describing the situation of

Jesus. Prior to this Jesus has had great success and has chosen his followers. Now Mark begins with an audacious statement from the crowd about Jesus having lost his mind. Matthew who normally takes up Marcan material (over ninety percent) does not do so with this first section, nor does Luke who follows Mark in over forty percent of the material. The translation of the *New Revised Standard Version* follows the older manuscripts (Alexandrian) and (Western) which read in the singular and thus have Jesus alone entering the house. The plural reading is less convincing for it is based on what was said in verses 17-19 which names the followers of Jesus (B. Metzger, *A Textual Commentary on the Greek New Testament*, New York United Bible Societies, 1971, p. 82).

Verse 21 has a Greek expression which is multivalent (*hoi par autou*) literally "those who were with him." Modern exegetes translate this as "his family or his brethren." In classic Greek this expression means ambassadors or envoys; in the book of Maccabees it can denote adherents or followers; in papyrus readings it means "neighbors," "friends," and "relatives." The context, however, suggests his "family" and not merely his friends or neighbors. Thus verse 21 should be considered when referring to Mary and Jesus' brothers and sisters or his extended family of cousins also called brothers and sisters. The family has heard about Jesus' activity and this draws them to where he and the crowds are so that they might "take hold of him" just as one making an arrest. The verb is that strong in its meaning! There is evidence of a deep personal concern on the part of the family for Jesus but no sympathy for his behavior or his activity of preaching, teaching, and exorcizing demons. In my estimation the verb "they were saying" seems to mean his family and not people in general were saying that "Jesus is besides himself," that is, he has gone mad. Henry Wansbrough points out that the words themselves can refer to the crowd, that is, it has gone wild or is crazy and frenzied. Perhaps, recalling the later Gospel of John, we can aver that Mark's bolder sense may have been the original tradition. In John 7:5 we read, "For not even his brothers believed in him" (see also the following: Jn 7:20; 8:48, 52; and 10:21) (H. Wansbrough,

A New Catholic Commentary on Scripture, New York: Nelson, 1975, p. 962).

V. Taylor states: "Moreover, the story of the true kindred of Jesus (3:31-35 which Mark has in mind in 3:19b-21), has an unmistakable atmosphere of tension, for which we account best if the family of Jesus were of the opinion expressed by *(elegen gar hoti ekseste)* 'he is out of his mind.' We conclude therefore that the subject of *elegon* is *hoi par autou"* (V. Taylor, *The Gospel According to Mark*, p. 237). It can mean that Jesus is considered to be mad in the sense of crazy. His mission and his vision have led him to be out of touch with reality and of his own limits.

Since we are concerned with the final pericope, I will not comment to any extent on the section called the collusion with Satan. There are parallels to it in Matthew 12:22-26 and Luke 11:14-18. This also pertains to the hypothetical "Q" (primarily made up of the "sayings of Jesus" and found in Lukan parallels with Matthew) wherein we know there is a situation concerning Jesus' expulsion of a demon from a dumb man. Thus an original apothegm or saying of Jesus is expanded by such sayings-material in Q. It, too, is the residue of a very early tradition. Taylor comments, "It reveals the fierce opposition to which the ministry of Jesus was exposed and His strong consciousness of being at death-grips with Satan and all his powers" (Taylor, p. 238). By saying that Jesus has Beelzebul means he is possessed by an evil spirit; the second charge is distinct and means that his exorcisms are done by the ruler of demons. The *New Jerome Biblical Commentary* has this to say: "'Possessed by Beelzebul': the first charge is that Jesus is possessed by a particular demon. Beelzebub is the name found in some ancient versions, but not in Gk. mss.; that form is based on 2 K 1:2, 'the lord of the flies.' Beelzebul is variously explained: 'the lord of the dung,' or 'the lord of the height or dwelling.' None of these is certain. 'By the chief of demons': the second charge is that Jesus' exorcisms took place through the mediation of Satan" (*NJBC*, 41:23, p. 604).

In the brief reference of Mark 3:27-30 which contains the parable or simile of Jesus about the strong man's house, we can say the phrase is characteristic of Jesus' manner of preaching, that is, refuting his opposition through clear and practical parables, similes, and sayings.

The only direct appearance of Mary in this Gospel is in 3:31-35. There is, as we will see, a reference to her name in Mark 6:3; this is, as we have said, the first reference to the name of Mary in the New Testament. Jesus is only identified through his heavenly Parent who is called the "Father" in this Gospel. Joseph is never mentioned. Jesus' only earthly parent is Mary (6:3). Jesus, not Joseph, is called the craftsman or carpenter in Mark's account. The absence of any mention of Joseph could suggest that he was already dead at this stage of the ministry of Jesus. Exegetes also consider the fact that this may have been an anti-Marian text in the sense that unbelievers could be stating that Jesus is illegitimate. This was an early anti-Christian polemic. Relevant to this interpretation is Jane Schaberg's book.[2]

Another interpretation, that of J.M. Robinson, suggests that Mark omitted the father of Jesus in order to underline that God alone is the Father of Jesus — just as he is the true Parent of the disciples once they have joined Jesus. Both pericopes are pointing to the spiritual relationship that is called for in discipleship rather than boasting about one's human origins.

Mark's placement of this pericope shows that he intends the scene to be connected with the earlier context in which Jesus is said to be "beside himself."

Before commenting on the individual lines of Mark 3:31-35, it will prove helpful for the rest of this study and those that follow to point out the importance of the Biblical Commission's instruction, *The Historical Truth of the Gospels*, of 1964.[3] An excellent methodology which consists in the three stages of Gospel development helps both the scholar and the student to move beyond a mere literal understanding of the Gospel texts to a more solid analysis of the development that took place. This instruction is particularly helpful in studying the Christology of the Gospels or for studies in Mariology which are closely related to Christology. These three stages are fully described in the instruction. A short summary of them includes the following:

(1) the actual historical words and deeds of Jesus as far as they can be affirmed of Jesus of Nazareth.

(2) the apostolic preaching and witnessing to these words and deeds which are faithfully explained "while taking into account their method of preaching and the circumstances in which their listeners found themselves" (*Historical Truth*, VIII).

(3) the work or writing of the Evangelists or sacred authors who as theologians or Christologists in their own right wrote their particular Gospel with specific purpose for a definite community of believers. It is they who gathered what they could from the above two stages and put it into the final form which we now have as the Gospels.

Keeping this all in mind as we proceed through any Gospel study, we now can approach the individual lines of Mark 3:31-35.

Verse 31: "Then (*kai*) his mother and his brothers came; and standing outside, they sent to him and called him." It is Mark, the Evangelist (note Stage 3), who redacts these introductory words from an independent tradition separate from 3:21-30. Several exegetes feel that this is the only incident in Jesus' life which reflects his historical situation with regard to his mother. I consider this a minimalist position which loses sight of such important historical events as the conception, birth, and early life which would necessitate contact with the one who gave Jesus that life.

Mark begins with his characteristic connective word *kai*, literally "and" which is translated here as "then." The mother of Jesus and his brothers are standing outside the house where Jesus is. They use an intermediary to send word to him to come out. We are already given a clue that Mark is working with several traditions for he only mentions the "brothers" and mother while in verse 32 the "sisters," too, are mentioned. Everything, however, centers on Jesus. Mark uses the personal pronoun (*autos*) four times in this introductory verse. Another Marcan characteristic is his use of the verbs, all of which, including the participle, are in a present tense: the historic present, a present tense used as a present perfect, and a present participle. Mark thus keeps the scene alive and dynamic.

Verse 32: "A crowd was sitting around him; and they said to him, 'Your mother and your brothers and sisters are outside, asking for you.'" We notice that the sisters and the crowd are now mentioned. Textual critics consider that the sisters were omitted from most manuscripts either because of an itacism, that is, an oversight in transcription, or because in verse 31 and 34 the sisters are not mentioned. If the words were interpolated they would have already appeared in line 31. There is also a conjecture that the sisters are added in order to harmonize the text with the climactic words of Jesus in verse 35. Bruce Metzger, an excellent text critic, says, "The shorter text preserved in the Alexandrian and Caesarean text-types should be adopted; the longer reading, perhaps of Western origin, crept into the text through mechanical expansion. From an historical point of view, it is extremely unlikely that Jesus' sisters would have joined in publicly seeking to check him in his ministry" (*A Textual Commentary on the Greek New Testament*, op. cit., p. 82). My own observation takes a different interpretation of this, namely, that Mark is working with two traditions, one of which included the sisters of Jesus. The message that the crowd gave to Jesus about their request probably passes from one to another till it reaches Jesus. Certainly, among this amorphous crowd there are already disciples who listen to the words of Jesus.

Verse 33: "And he replied, 'Who are my mother and my brothers?'"

This is a common way for Jesus to reply, that is, with another question. This expression is Septuagintal and is very prevalent in the Gospels. It is the pivot of the narrative and accounts for this incident being remembered. Vincent Taylor comments, "It is difficult not to find a tone of disappointment in the question, the recognition of a want of sympathy on the part of the family at Nazareth. The fact that it is consistent with tender care for kinsmen need not be doubted" (V. Taylor, op. cit., p. 264).

These lines are difficult for us (in the Catholic tradition) who have such a reverence for the person of Mary. The question and the attitude of the family of Jesus contradict the ethos found in the Infancy Narratives about the Virgin Mary.

Verse 34: "And looking at those who sat around him, he said, 'Here are my mother and my brothers!'" These lines indicate the searching look of Jesus as in Mark 3:5.

Verse 35: "Whoever does the will of God is my brother and sister and mother." This very saying of Jesus (*ipsissima verba Jesu*) could have come from the lips of Jesus of Nazareth (Stage 1).[4] Jesus like the teachers of Judaism places emphasis on doing the will of God; he sets family relationships on a new plane in which the ties of common obedience to God are superior to the blood ties of a natural family. These words give us a glimpse of the personal aspects of Jesus' envisioning of the Kingdom of God. It has a communitarian dimension and the following of Jesus as well as the formation of a Marcan community would lead to bringing others into this family of God precisely because these disciples were focused on doing the will of God. Mark's community is the true family which listens to Jesus' word and accomplishes the will of God.

The Christology of Chapter 3 of Mark

In chapter three, only two titles are used for Jesus. (Normally, it is first through a study of the titles of Jesus that one comes to know the Christology of a given evangelist.) In Mark 3:7 the name *Jesus* is the title which underlies all of the happenings and sayings of the chapter. There is but one exception in Mark 3:11, one of the so-called Messianic secret passages, "And whenever the unclean spirits beheld him, they fell down before him and cried out, 'You are the Son of God.'"

The other references to Jesus are simply the pronouns and possessive adjectives which refer to Jesus. It is clear that the Christology of Mark in this third chapter, and especially in our pericope, is one which centers on Jesus of Nazareth — perhaps, the best way of naming Jesus when we are referring to Stage 1 of the Gospels. Of course, it is Mark who is the narrator. He is presenting the reader or listener with the time of the earthly and not resurrected Jesus. The relationship of Jesus to his mother, brothers, and sisters is set within a true family setting in which a mother's concern for her children would be at stake [5] This seems to fit their concern, namely, that his activity and preaching may be giving the wrong impression to the listeners about his natural origins. They are coming to rescue their own reputation and privacy as a family as well as to rescue Jesus. Their relative, Jesus, has "gone out of his mind" (Mk 3:21). If so, this is the incident that happened in the real historical life of Jesus in which Mary had a part. But, it also could be Mark's literary creation as well. The words of Jesus then would fit the theology of Mark's concern for his own community. Both the narrative and the saying were intended by Mark to give us an example about one of the ordinary occurrences in the life of Jesus. The context of a mother and relatives coming to rescue their family reputation and their privacy is quite normal and realistic. One can easily imagine this same situation in many a family today. What is, however, uncharacteristic, is the response of Jesus who rejects their anxious concerns. He, instead, gives value to the presence and attitude of the ones surrounding him, the crowd. He offsets family ties, and possibly the selfish concerns of his brothers, sisters, and mother. What would be the more human response is not heard in the words of Jesus. He spiritualizes the whole situation by speaking of the will of God and thereby discovering a transcendent family relation to one another through doing God's will. This would seem to meet the criteria for the authenticity of the teachings of Jesus (Norman Perrin, *Rediscovering the Teachings of Jesus*, New York, Harper, p. 39); and yet, paradoxically, "doing the will of God" is the fulfiling of the Torah, and thereby, a most profound Jewish reaction on the part of Jesus.

The Eschatological Family of Jesus

In the ecumenical study of *Mary in the New Testament*, Paul Donfried comments on verse 35: "When v. 35 is considered in itself, it tells us who constitute Jesus' family — a family that for want of a better term we may call his 'eschatological family,' i.e., the family called into being by Jesus' proclamation of the kingdom. This eschatological family (brother, sister, and mother) consists of those who do God's will" (*MNT*, p. 53). We can sketch the scene in concentric circles. Jesus of Nazareth, the Jesus of history is in the center — his true eschatological family is the crowd of people encircling him and listening to him, while on the outside of the circle is his natural family. In the reality of the reign of God Jesus proclaims that those who listen and hear him are his mother, brother, and sister, while those anxiously concerned about the family reputation find themselves outside the circle.

The Christological meaning of this passage is the challenge that springs from the lips of the Jesus of history telling us that family ties and relationships are of secondary importance when it comes to the primary relationship we are to have with God and Jesus, the agent Revealer of God. The strength of Jesus the Jew comes in his assertion of separation from his natural family when it comes to the primacy of doing the will of God. There is an echo of this in Luke's scene of the Finding of the Child Jesus in the Temple when he says, "Why were you searching for me, did you not know I must be in my Father's house?" (Lk 2:49). Likewise, on that occasion, Mary and Joseph "... did not understand what he said to them" (Lk 2:50). This type of detachment from the family is even more radical and demanding for one bound to the Semitic ties of relationship. The Christology of relationship calls forth a response to leave aside anything that is bound up with an over-concerned family attitude, or a selfish fixation on one's reputation. It rather consists in the wisdom of Jesus, that is, doing the will of God. Sometimes actual separation or a "breaking-away" may be called for while responding to the message of Jesus. One is not left alone; one discovers that God cares for one's family which has new brothers, mother, and sisters. Jesus in Luke 's Gospel will express this idea in almost a harsh way, "Whoever comes to me and does not hate father and mother, wife and children, brothers and sisters, yes, and even life itself, cannot be my disciple" (Lk 14:26). B.H. Branscomb says: "The reign of God was not in Jesus' mind an abstract concept or a theological necessity, but a personal fellowship with men and women who would do the will of God" (*Commentary on St. Mark's Gospel*, Moffat Commentaries, London: Hodder and Stoughton, 1952).

Scholars agree that the point of the passage is to show clearly who really make up the eschatological family of God. The point is not to exclude Jesus' natural family; in fact, we would hope they eventually did believe in Jesus and his message. In harmony with our pericope is the saying of Jesus in Mark 10:29-30: "Truly, I tell you, there is no one who has left house or brothers or sisters or mother or father or children or fields, for my sake and for the sake of the good news, who will not receive a hundredfold now in this age — houses and brothers and sisters and mothers and children and fields with persecutions — and in the final age to come eternal life."

Mark 6:1-6a

We can now move on to the second passage in Mark which treats of Jesus and his relatives. Here his brothers are named and his mother is named but they are not present. The context is different. No longer are the crowds favorably responding to Jesus. The setting is not a house (Mk 3:20) but a synagogue. The titles used for Jesus in this narrative are his name and "prophet." The Christology again is a "low Christology" and probably springs from the first stage of the Jesus tradition in the Gospels. From such a perspective, it is a Christology that is parallel and consonant with the pericope just studied, Mark 3:31-35.

In their astonishment, the people from Jesus' own country — the highlands of Galilee — ask: " 'Is not this the carpenter, the son of Mary and brother of James and Joses and Judas and Simon, and are not his sisters here with us?' And they took offense at him" (Mk 6:3).

The pericope is, like the former one, an apothegm in which the proverb of verse 4 is emphasized: "Prophets are not without honor, except in their hometown, and among their own kin, and in their own house." The narrative portions seem to be Marcan constructions; the proverb is not original to Jesus. Hence, the entire scene is a Marcan creation which could even be based on our first pericope, Mark 3:31-35. In fact, the proverb contains the reference to house and the mention of relatives. What is missing from this scene is the concentric pattern of chapter 3; instead, the pattern is linear: "His disciples followed him" (Mk 6:1). The synagogue setting merely arouses the astonishment of the people and raises more questions about who Jesus is and about his teaching and ministry. In turn, Jesus marvels at the lack of trust and at the unbelief of his own townspeople.

Again the neighbors of Jesus and his own townspeople are concerned about his non-conformist behavior. How could one whom we know to be a carpenter, and who is the son of Mary, teach and work mighty deeds? Mark is not only showing the conflict of Jesus among his own, but is also stressing the humanness of Jesus in his own community. Mark's Gospel presents Jesus as a normal human being to offset any supernaturalist attitude toward Jesus in Mark's community. Was not this the argument of those who first began the study of Mark in quest for the historical Jesus? They had hoped to find only the Jesus of history within this Gospel (G.W. Lathrop, *Who Shall Describe His Origin? Tradition and Redaction in Mark 6:1-6a*. Dissertation. Nijmegen: Catholic University, 1969).

Mark's description of the villagers and of the brothers and sisters of Jesus, and even of Mary his mother, confirms what we saw earlier. The relatives of Jesus are of the same opinion as their neighbors. They are shocked and concerned that Jesus is different. He was trained as a carpenter or craftsman, what business does he have teaching in our synagogue? Why should an ordinary Galilean assume the role of a prophet both in speech and healing people? Jesus is no different than they are. Why all this attention? Perhaps he is crazy, that is, possessed.

The pericope is a shadow of the one we saw in Mark 3:31-35. But here in 6:1-6a Jesus is not received by anyone — except to the equally shadowy reference to "those who followed him." His word and his works are not received; there is no response to the communication he offers; as a result, Jesus could do no miracles in his homeland because of their lack of faith. His trust in God as Parent is natural, while theirs is an attitude of distrust and skepticism; it is forced and immature.

Who Is Jesus?

Are there any new dimensions to the Christology within this pericope which go beyond what was said in Mark 3:31-35? In the overall theological perspective of Mark there is an increasing disclosure of who Jesus is. Perhaps the use of the questions in 6:1-3 is a technique of Mark to bring out who Jesus is. In contrast to the former scene, now the possible title of Jesus as prophet is presented. This is not unlike the unfolding of the titles of Jesus which take place in chapter one of John's Gospel (Jn 1:35-51). This would then indicate a progression in understanding who Jesus is as a prophet.

There is also the term *skandalizomai* ("and they took offense at him," Mk 6:3b). After 70 C.E. this term was a specialized expression for describing the effect of Jesus' death upon his own nation Israel (cf. the earlier use of *skandalon* in Rm 9:33; 1 Cor 1:23; Gal 5:11). This is definitely at the heart of Mark's Christology which is bound up with a Passion-Death theme in the Cross and in which the tragedy of Jesus' rejection by his own people is brought out. The term may reveal in Mark, already at this point in the ministry of Jesus, a post-resurrectional insight similar to what John would say in his prologue: "He came to what was his own, and his own people did not accept him" (Jn 1:11).

Mark 6:1-6a. Some exegetical observations on each line:

Verse 1: Jesus returns to his native land or hometown. The fact that the disciples are following him shows him as a teacher, a rabbi. He already has been teaching with authority (*exousia*).

Verse 2: Once the Sabbath has come, Jesus preaches in the synagogue. There now is a current of dissatisfaction among his listeners about the origin of his teaching, the nature of his wisdom, as well as the mighty works or healings he has done.

The *dia ton cheiron autou* (being done by his hands) refers to the healing touch of his hand. The hostility is not of the same intensity as that experienced in 3:22-30. Matthew abbreviates Mark at this point while Luke vividly describes the scene and shows the attention of the listeners (Mt 13:53-58; Lk 4:20-30).

Verse 3: The tone is perceptibly different from that of verse 2. The culmination is the fact "they were scandalized by him" or as the *New Revised Standard Version* has: "they took offense at him."

Verse 4: R. Bultmann believes that these words of Jesus were constructed around a common saying that is present also in the Oxyrhynchus papyrus 1.5: "A prophet is not acceptable in his own country and a physician effects no cures among those who know him." Mark constructs his more complicated double parable out of this simpler one. As is usual, Bultmann affirms this is secondary material composed by the final redactor out of the missionary experience of the Church (cf. Jn 4:44 and Mt 13:57). The proverb is very common; Jesus is called a prophet in all four Gospels (cf. R. Bultmann, *History of the Synoptic Tradition*, New York: Harper & Row, 2nd ed., 1968, p. 31).

Verses 5, 6a: This passage is one of the boldest statements about Jesus for it says that he could not do something. Notice also Mark in 13:32 has Jesus say, "But about that day or hour no one knows, neither the angels in heaven, nor the Son, but only the Father." No parallel to our passage is found in Luke 4:16-30, and Matthew recasts it into a softened statement (Mt 13:58).

The expression "the son of Mary" has no parallel elsewhere in the New Testament. It is not the custom to identify a son through his mother's name; in fact, it is usually an insult (cf. Jg 11:1ff.). Could it be that Mark is unfamiliar with the tradition of the Virgin Birth? Did this phrase belong to the original text? Matthew 13:55 has a clear identification of Jesus and his family. As we have pointed out, more detail indicates a later tradition. See also such references in Luke 4:22 and John 6:42. There are some manuscripts of Mark that are closer to what Matthew says; for example, Papyrus #45 identifies Joseph as the father and also as the "carpenter." Origen also argues against Celsus that Jesus is described as an artisan in any of the Gospels familiar to him. Could the original reading be: "the son of the carpenter and of Mary"? Could it be that Mark wrcte "the son of the carpenter" and that an early scribe replaced this reading by saying Jesus was the "carpenter" and added the "son of Mary"?

The Brothers and Sisters of Jesus

> (Cf. Mk 3:31-35; 6:3; Mt 13:55; Ac 12:17; 15:13; 21:18;
> 1 Cor 15:7; Gal 1:19; 2:9, 12; Jm 1:1; Jude 1)

These texts propose a difference of interpretation among Catholic exegetes and all other believers whether Christian or Jewish. To my knowledge, I have not found other Christians accepting the Catholic interpretation which would say the "brothers and sisters" of Jesus are male and female cousins of Jesus. Hence, brother and sister are being used in the more extended sense as is the case in African and Arab countries.

The differences of cpinion are practically the same as the three earliest interpretations given to these relatives of Jesus. In all cases, there is the question of whether Mary remained virgin throughout her life and whether Jesus was an only son. Interestingly enough, the three opinions stem from the same period of 380-385 C.E. The hypotheses are divided into the following:

1. The Helvidian (Helvidius, around 380 C.E.) which says the *adelphoi* were blood brothers to Jesus; so, too, the sisters. Tertullian also has this opinion.

2. The Epiphanian (Epiphanius, 382 C.E.) which maintains that the brothers and sisters are children of Joseph from a former marriage. Origen also agrees with this.

3. The Hieronymian (Jerome, 383 C.E.) maintains they were cousins of Jesus, the sons and daughters of another Mary, the wife of Clopas, and sister to Mary of Nazareth, the mother of Jesus.

This topic is adequately presented in *Mary in the New Testament*, but the classic study of the texts is that of Joseph Blinzler, *Die Brüder und Schwestern Jesu*. After a careful study of all the texts, he comes to his own conclusion which is very close to that of Jerome: "The so-called brothers and sisters of Jesus were male and female cousins. The relationship of Simon and Jude with Jesus occurs through their father Clopas and thus these were of the lineage of David; their mother's name is not known. The mother of the Lord's brothers, James and Joses, was a different Mary from the Lord's mother. Either she or her husband were related to the family of Jesus, but the nature of the relationship cannot be ascertained."[6]

Conclusion to Mark's Imaging of Mary

After reading the texts of Mark, is it possible to have a positive image of Mary in relation to her son Jesus? As we have seen, most exegetes think not. Catholic scholars and ecclesial documents tend to avoid any mention of the Marcan pericopes. Several Catholic exegetes assert a "virginal" reference in Mark 6:3 where Mary alone is considered the natural parent of Jesus, but we have seen that in the polemic against Jesus this same text could be used to indicate illegitimacy. We have seen evidence that the early scribes may have altered this text. What, then, can we say about Mary in Mark's Gospel? Was she, too, one of the unbelievers among his relatives? Did she lack a comprehension of his message as do the disciples and followers of Jesus in this Gospel? Mark gives us no more than a silhouette of this woman and does not deal with our questions. She is realistically presented as a devout mother who is concerned about the welfare of her family, its reputation, and, of course, her son, Jesus. She is on the periphery in the scene from 3:31-35; she is merely mentioned by name in Mark 6:3. There is too little data here to say anything about her definitively. It is really a true silhouette without any dimension or depth. From the fact that the other evangelists use these traditions of Mark and add to them, we will come to see her as a believer and disciple of the Lord, but Mark does not indicate this in his Gospel. With more recent studies on these pericopes, it is best to say that the passages in themselves do not exclude her from eventually belonging to the eschatological family of Jesus. Any thoughts on her, and for that matter, any exegesis on the lines in which she appears in Mark will usually depend on the authority the scholars allot to later Church insights. For my part, the call to believe in the message of Jesus and to follow him is strongly suggested in these two passages.

Endnotes

1. Bertrand Buby, "A Christology of Relationship in Mark," *Biblical Theology Bulletin* 10, Oct. 1980, pp. 149-154.

2. Jane Schaberg, *The Illegitimacy of Jesus: A Feminist Theological Interpretation of the Infancy Narratives*, San Francisco: Harper, 1987.

3. *The Historical Truth of the Gospels: The 1964 Instruction of the Biblical Commission*, Glen Rock, N.J.: Paulist, 1964. Commentary by Joseph A. Fitzmyer, S.J.

4. Robert W. Funk, Roy W. Hoover, and the Jesus Seminar, *The Five Gospels: The Search for the Authentic Words of Jesus, What did Jesus Really say*, New York: Macmillan, 1993, p. 53. This is the most recent study on the words of Jesus. It takes a minimalist position.

5. Victor H. Matthews, "Female Voices: Upholding the Honor of the Household," *Biblical Theology Bulletin* 24, Spring 1994, no. 1, pp. 8-15.

6. Joseph Blinzler, *Die Brüder und Schwestern Jesu*, SBS 21, Stuttgart: Katholisches Bibelwerk, 1967.

Chapter Three

MATTHEW'S SKETCH OF MARY

Chapters 1 and 2; 12:46-50; and 13:53-58

With the Infancy Narratives of Matthew and Luke, we enter into a development of the Gospels which goes beyond the simple and direct proclamation of Mark's Passion Narrative. Mark had combined the latter with the ministry of Jesus seen in the unraveling of the Messianic Secret: Jesus Son of Man becomes Son of God in the mystery of his rejection, suffering, and death.

Matthew belongs to the third generation of Christians and Jews who believed in Jesus (80-85 C.E.). The composition of his Gospel takes place fifty years after the death of Jesus and at least ten years after the Gospel of Mark. Instead of the imminent expectation of Jesus' return, we see Matthew working with the concerns of his own community (probably in the Syrian region). Questions are now being asked about Jesus that go far beyond the Marcan community's concerns, such questions as: What were his origins? Who are his ancestors? Where was he born? What do the Hebrew Scriptures say about Jesus? Of whom was he born? Why was it so? Matthew in a carefully constructed Gospel attempts to answer these questions and to continue teaching his community through the words and deeds of Jesus and the example of the disciples of Jesus.

Matthew is also confronted with a difficult socio-religious dimension. His community was on the verge of dividing against itself because of a renewed Judaism, a restored Pharisaical synagogue which was flourishing and was quite attractive to the Jewish members of the Matthean community. The synagogue was, so to speak, just across the street from the church (Matthew is the only Gospel to use the term "Church" in 16:18 and 18:17). The influx of ¹Greek-speaking converts who were non-Jewish led to a crisis of identification among the Jewish Christians who belonged, were more seasoned, and probably more generous to the community. They were seriously tempted to leave the Church and to return to the Synagogue while still professing their belief in Jesus. The beautiful structures, rituals, prescriptions, and symbols of the Torah attracted them to return to what they once knew and fully appreciated. Matthew's Gospel is a delicate, well-thought-out plan for helping both parts of his community. The community which was divided against itself would, through this Gospel, remain faithful to the teachings of the Apostles and their Rabbi, Jesus. Matthew succeeded both theologically and pastorally in keeping the community together and helped it grow into a deeper commitment to Jesus and his words of life.

Matthew reflected both upon the Torah and the Gospel of Mark (of which he used over ninety percent or 600 of Mark's 677 verses). He reconstructs from the Torah and the traditions known to him Jesus' Jewish origins and the role of Mary of Nazareth in Jesus' conception and birth.

Matthew, therefore, besides being faithful to the Christian traditions known from Mark, expands the Gospel through a profound reflection on the Hebrew Scriptures. He does this primarily and paradigmatically in his Infancy Narrative (chapters one and two). He also searched for more recollections and memoirs of Jesus and his "sayings" in and among the members of his community. His own pastoral and theological considerations became a part of his Gospel as well.

In this study we have only to comment on the first two chapters of Matthew and the parallel passages from Mark where Mary was remembered or mentioned explicitly. This chapter will consist of four parts: (1) the genealogy or origins of Jesus, (2) the

manner of his birth, (3) the mother and child, and (4) the recollections of Mary taken from Mark's Gospel.

1. The Genealogy or Origins of the Messiah, Jesus Christ (Mt 1:1-17)

Matthew's introductory line, like that of the other Evangelists,
is of great importance for understanding and interpreting his
Gospel. He starts by telling us about the "birth record" of Jesus. It
equally could be called the book of the origins of Jesus as Messiah.
That the emphasis is on the birth is made clear by verse 18 which
takes up with the manner of Jesus' birth after having completed his
genealogy. The Christological emphasis is on the Messiahship of
Jesus precisely because he is a son of David. This Messiahship is
extended to all peoples because he is also a son of Abraham, the
parent symbol of all believers.

The genealogy is not original with Matthew. He borrows
these names from several of the genealogical accounts in the
Hebrew Scriptures. It is both a segmented and symbolic genealogy.
"Segmented genealogies in the ancient East were generally not for
conveying historical information but for determining domestic,
political-juridical, and religious matters" (*NJBC*, 2:7, p. 13).

These birth records are called *Toledoth* or "begettings" in the
Hebrew Scriptures and Matthew uses several of them to achieve his
purpose (see Gn 5:1; Rt 4:18-22; 1 Ch 2:10-15). The "begetting
pattern" is used throughout Matthew's Gospel with the same formula: "A begot B." The Davidic lineage is especially emphasized.
The verb form which is used (*gennan*) underlines the male principle
of generation and can be translated "to be the father of.' However,
the paradoxical surprise is that Matthew introduces five important
women, four of whom are named in order to show that God's ways
are not the stereotyped ways of a male-dominated culture and
religion.

In general, people are not interested in reading or listening to
this genealogy, but it is important and was significant for Matthew's
community in identifying who Jesus is and his legitimacy within

Judaism. Moreover, it is one of the ways in which the Messianic claim is verified in Jesus from Matthew's purpose and point of view. There is the following sagacious sentence in the *NJBC*: "Monotony and inconsistencies of this literary form must not blind a modern reader to its indispensable role, replaced nowadays by parish and civil record offices, in vindicating legitimacy of both family and function" (*NJBC* 23:10).

Matthew collects the names from the Hebrew Scriptures but sets them in three stages each consisting of fourteen names. This is where some of the symbolism he uses through numbers appears; the name of David is equivalent to fourteen in the Hebrew language. This is determined by the numerical value of the consonants D = 4, Wav = 6, D = 4, or David. Matthew certainly was aware that he could not go back to Abraham with so few names, for they are insufficient in themselves to bridge the gaps of so many generations adding up to almost 800 to 1000 years; their purpose is to assure the reader that Jesus is of the Messianic line. To show the extraordinary birth of Jesus, Matthew has the five women enter the genealogy to extend this Messiahship to all peoples and to illustrate through salvation history that God works in unexpected and surprising ways. Matthew will continue to use the symbolism of numbers which are considered sacred, for example, five, seven, ten, twelve. There are the five dreams in this Gospel, the five great discourses, the five loaves. Sevens are indicative of fulfillment or completion. Fourteen is made up of two sevens, etc.

The introductory verse, therefore, frames the genealogy presenting Jesus Christ as the descendant of David and Abraham. David represents the human aspect of the Messiah, the promises made to David by God, and the rootedness of Jesus in Judaism. Abraham indicates the line of faith for all believers, Jew or Gentile, male or female. Through Abraham the spiritual lineage is symbolized. This also explains the importance of the women who represent the spiritual and faith dimension of Jesus Christ. Mary his mother is the fifth and culminating person in this genealogy and it is through the action of the Spirit that Jesus is born of her.

More recently, Jack D. Kingsbury sees in the introductory expression *biblos geneseos* (birth record or book of origins) a way of understanding not only the genealogy but also the events which follow up to 4:16, the verse prior to the proclamation of Jesus: "From that time Jesus began to proclaim, 'Repent, for the kingdom of heaven has come near.'"[1]

Let us return then to the five women who break up the usual pattern of the genealogy: verse 3: from Tamar; verse 5: from Rahab and from Ruth; verse 6: from the wife of Uriah (Bathsheba) and the culmination, "Jesus, who was *born of Mary*" (verse 16).

In the history of interpretation there have been four proposals as to why Matthew introduces the women: first, to show that Jesus is the Savior of all, even sinners. The women are regarded by some as sinners, yet both in the New Testament and in Judaism they are also considered heroines or saints. Mary, of course, would be excluded from the negative aspect of this proposal. Secondly, the women are considered to be foreigners, again, except Mary. This is Luther's interpretation. Thirdly, all women, including Mary are considered to be in an unusual marital relationship; there is something irregular in their union with their partners. They also show extraordinary cooperation as instruments of God's power or God's Spirit. More recently, Marshall Johnson introduces a fourth proposal: the conscious refuting of attacks against the legitimacy of Jesus' birth.[2] There is also the feminist exegesis of these texts which points out the dangerous situation of all five women who are placed outside of the patriarchal family structures. "The women's presence functions, therefore, as a critique of patriarchy and introduces a point of tension into the narrative that must guide the reader as the story unfolds" (Elaine Mary Wainwright, *Towards a Feminist Critical Reading of the Gospel According to Matthew*, New York: de Gruyter, 1991, p. 68). Michael Crosby says, "Thus through Joseph the patriarchal line continued. But through the woman, Mary, a new house-ordering would be established in the life and work of Jesus" (M. Crosby, *House of Disciples: Church, Economics, and Justice in Matthew*. Maryknoll: Orbis, 1988, p. 87).

2. The Manner of His Birth

Matthew 1:16: "Mary, of whom Jesus was born, who is called the Messiah."

Matthew 1:16 contains the first mention of Mary in Matthew's Gospel. It is important to see this mention of Mary as his own tradition which in this part of his Gospel is in no way dependent on Mark. The manner in which Mary is mentioned already points to the event of Jesus' being born of a virgin. The remaining verses of chapter one will confirm this interpretation of verse 16.

Mary enters as the fifth and final woman in the genealogy. She is presented in an entirely different way from the two patterns Matthew has used both for the male ancestors and for the women: Tamar, Rahab, Ruth, and the wife of Uriah. Mary is the lawful wife of Joseph. There is no irregularity within the marriage; however, the manner in which the Messiah is to be born is of the Spirit. Matthew links the physical birth of the Messiah to his mother and not to Joseph. The next pericope is a marvelously constructed one in which the genealogy and the birth of Jesus are carefully demonstrated.

Matthew 1:18-25

This paragraph is one of the most creative in Matthew, both in its theological purpose and in its manner of presentation. It is more than just a prolonged footnote to the genealogy just presented. It serves almost as a showpiece for the unfolding of the whole Gospel and complements the final paragraph of Matthew (Mt. 28:16-20) in which Jesus continues till the end of time to be "with us" (Emmanuel).

Before going into any details about this pericope, Raymond Brown's succinct and important comment on Mt 1:18-25 can help us realize the difficulties involved in interpreting this passage:

"It should be added here that the joining of the genealogy to 1:18-25, the presence therein of two pre-Matthean episodes (angelic dream appearance; annunciation of birth), and the incorporation of a fulfillment citation makes 1:18-25 the most complicated section in the whole infancy narrative — the one with the heaviest Matthean rewriting and the one whose pre-history is the most difficult to determine" (*Birth of the Messiah*, p. 119).

Verse 18: Matthew carefully links this verse to the beginning of his Gospel by speaking of the birth of Jesus who is named the Christ (Messiah or Ano nted One). The reason for the genealogy will be seen in the first part of this verse . . ."His mother Mary had been betrothed to Joseph." The virginal conception which was hinted at in verse 16 now becomes explicit . . ."it was found that she was with child through the Holy Spirit." These phrases contain what will be the mystery of Jesus Christ: he is legally a descendant of David through Joseph; he is likewise, through the operation of the Holy Spirit in the virgin Mary, Jesus, the Savior. The latter implies He is God's Son because of the Holy Spirit. This parallels one of the oldest creedal statements about Jesus which Paul uses in the Epistle to the Romans. Paul is probably dependent on an earlier tradition for it: "the gospel concerning his Son, who was descended from David according to the flesh and was declared to be Son of God with power according to the spirit of holiness (or Spirit) by resurrection from the dead, Jesus Christ our Lord" (Rm 1:3-4). Both in Matthew and in Romans we have the tension of Jesus being a son of David according to the flesh and a Son of God according to the Spirit.

Verse 19: Joseph is the center of the pericope beginning at this point. He is just, that is, upright in the sense of being a wholesome and integrated man who follows the revelation of the Torah in its fullest sense. How will he deal with Mary's pregnancy which is not of his doing? This tension within the text presents three different lines of interpretation probably dependent on the way the word *dikaios* or "just" is interpreted. The three different explanations are: (1) Joseph is just in the sense of being compassionate and kind towards Mary. He is to take the most lenient way of easing himself out of the predicament of Mary's pregnancy, while observing the law. Thus she will be released from their betrothal. (2) Joseph is somehow made aware of God's plan of salvation to be accomplished in Mary and stands in great respect and awe before the mystery. He does not consider himself worthy to be a part of it, therefore, he will separate himself from Mary. (3) He is just in the sense of being fully observant of the Law, therefore, Mary is to be divorced. Brown explains it well, "In this interpretation, while Joseph's sense of obedience to the Law forced him in conscience to divorce Mary, his unwillingness to expose her to public disgrace led him to proceed without accusation of serious crime. He was upright *but* also merciful" (*Birth of the Messiah*, p. 127). Though this is the interpretation favored by most exegetes there is a long ecclesial tradition for the awe and respect of Joseph in the face of Mary's mystery or secret that he becomes aware of. The third interpretation proceeds from strict exegesis and through the historical critical method. The second issues from a profound reflection on the biblical theology implied in the text. Perhaps, it is best to work with all three interpretations before reaching one's own opinion on the meaning of the text.

Verse 20: This line resolves all three of the above interpretations for it shows that God takes the initiative and reveals to Joseph in a dream through the "angel of the Lord" (another expression for God) the mystery of the child who is begotten in Mary through the Holy Spirit. This begetting is totally different from those mentioned in the genealogy; the woman, likewise, mentioned is different from the other four in the sense she is legally betrothed to Joseph and is in no way opposing the initiative of God. Joseph through the dream is being called to do the same by accepting the child legally as his own. In a sense, he is being asked to say "yes" to what Mary already has said "yes." The suggestion of the angel that Joseph take Mary to his home would be the completion of their betrothal. She would be his lawful wife and her son would be legitimate according to the Law. Both Mary and Joseph are thus intimately bound to the mystery of the Messiah's birth in the mystery of their marriage. Grace, once again, builds on nature. Joseph accepts the initiative and surprising revelation of God while asleep. A dream clarifies for him the integrating factors of what seemed so broken, so perplexing, and so troublesome. What Luke has happening to Mary in broad daylight, in Matthew takes place in the darkness of the night for Joseph. The Annunciations are similar in their reality and their meaning.

Verse 21: The name of the child is to be Jesus (Joshua) for "he will save his people from their sins." Matthew uses the universal term "people" since both the descendants of David and those of Abraham will be saved through Jesus. This verse fits well the universalism of the closing lines of Matthew. Jesus will be the Exodus Event for all peoples, not just Israel. His name follows upon Joshua who succeeded Moses and led the people of Israel to their safety, that is, to their salvation in the Land. It is Joseph who is to name the child, Jesus. Thus the one word which he is indicated to speak is God's revelation in Jesus. The otherwise silent Joseph has broken his silence.

Verse 22 is Matthew's introduction to the first prophetic text of his Gospel. "Spoken by the Lord through the prophet . . ." is also an expression common to the Hebrew Scriptures as a way of showing where God explicitly gives revelation usually through a prophetic voice. Matthew, of course, is referring to Isaiah 7:14 which follows in verse 23. In the Infancy Narrative, Matthew will use the prophecy formula five times. It occurs six other times in his Gospel. It may be indicative of how Matthew used existing traditions and then reflected upon them in the light of the Hebrew Scriptures, especially the Nebiim or Prophetic parts. A parallel method is used in the Qumran community where texts of the Scriptures were used to show what is being accomplished in the present. It is a midrashic type of interpretation based on the simple (*pesher*) reading of the text and adapting it to the present needs of the community. A modern homily based on the Scriptures is similar in scope. Matthew would thus be profoundly studying, reflecting, and gathering texts to understand the traditions he was working with. We could call Matthew 1:18-25 a type of Christian *midrash*, recalling that the word *midrash* comes from the verb meaning to search carefully (*drsh*).

Verse 23: Matthew's first citation of the Isaiah 7:14 text is

imposed on what he has written; however, he does this intention-
ally. It gives us the clue to understanding Matthew's ten other
fulfillment citations with an introductory formula as in verse 22. It
will also become, in the earliest traditions after the New Testament
(Justin, Irenaeus, Chrysostom, Jerome, etc.), the main text for a
polemicism against those who deny the virgin birth. What is more
important is that the concept of a virgin birth existed prior to the
writing of Matthew. He uses the text from Isaiah primarily in a
Christological manner while at the same time not contradicting
anything he has said about the unusual status of Mary (see verses 16,
18, 20, 25). Matthew may have also had access to several versions
of Isaiah for parts of his citation are based on the Septuagint, others
on a text similar to the later Massoretic text in Hebrew, and still
others similar to the Aramaic texts. We cannot force Matthew into
using the texts of the Hebrew Scriptures in the scientific and
historical critical way that today's exegetes employ. Matthew is
writing from and for a community of faith that lived in the ethos and
spirit of these texts as a way of life that went beyond literalism or
historicism. To uncover the intention of Matthew one also has to
work within the faith dimension implied in his own purpose. A
history of salvation is being conveyed in the opening chapters of
Matthew. Emmanuel is the name given to the child in the prophecy
and Matthew adds its meaning "God is with us." This is the only
direct use of the title in reference to Christ, but in 18:20 and 28:20
it is implied in the context.

Verse 24: Joseph consciously then confirms his righteousness
(*dikaiosyne*) in obeying the word of God's messenger. By taking Mary
into his home the marriage is legally completed and the child to be
born will be named by Joseph and accepted as his own. This system
of adoption is quite counter-culture to our own, but helps us to
understand the purpose of the genealogy and the birth narrative in
Matthew's Gospel.

Verse 25: Joseph names Jesus. In Luke it will be Mary who calls
her son Jesus. Both parents had this privilege as can be seen both
from the Hebrew Scriptures as well as in the account of the birth of

John the Baptist in Luke's Gospel. The final difficulty for readers in this verse is the translation of the Greek conjunction *heos* meaning "until." In the Greek it does not mean that Joseph therefore had marital relations with Mary after the birth of Jesus. As it is used here, it looks merely to the time of the birth of Jesus and not to what happens afterwards. This is easily seen in a similar use of *heos* in the account of Michal, the daughter of Saul. "And Michal the daughter of Saul had no child until the day of her death" (2 S 6:23 in the Septuagint).

3. *The Mother and Child*

Chapter 2 of Matthew

In this study we are primarily interested in the texts referring to Mary. Without commenting then on the birth of Jesus in Bethlehem and the visit of the Magi, we come to verse 11: "And entering the house, they saw the child with Mary his mother. . . ." The relationship between Jesus and Mary in all of chapter two will be that of a child to his mother. We notice that Mary is in Joseph's home in Bethlehem which is David's first town of his kingship. The scene also shows us a great difference in some of the details about the child's birth in Matthew and Luke.

What is noteworthy is that the first Gentiles to see Jesus also see him with his mother Mary. They offer their gifts and pay homage to him since he is the Messiah King. Father Viviano makes this insightful remark: "The magi offer a model of sound Mariology as worshippers of Christ in a Marian context" (*NJBC*, 42:12, p. 636).

As chapter two continues, we find that the next pericope dealing with Herod's attempt to destroy the newborn King of the Jews also has Jesus in relationship to his mother. Joseph serves as the "protector" of the child and his mother in 2:13-14; 2:20, 21 where the phrase "the child and his mother" appears.

The flight into Egypt continues to remind us that Matthew has both Moses and the Exodus Event in mind as he recounts the story of Jesus. R.E. Brown in his short epilogue on Matthew's Infancy Narrative says, "Of course, Matthew could have written an impersonal summary of Israel's history; but he chose to make the preparation more intimate by having Jesus relive that history. This infancy story then becomes as integral for Jesus' ministry as the infancy and youth of Moses (and the genealogy) in Exodus 1-6 were for Moses' ministry (*Birth*, p. 231).

4. Matthew's Parallels to Mark's Marian Passages

The final pericopes to be studied in reference to Mary are the parallel accounts that Matthew has to Mark. These are Jesus' true relatives in Matthew 12:46-50 (Mk 3:31-35) and Jesus' rejection at Nazareth in Matthew 13:53-58 (Mk 6:1-6a). Most exegetes posit a dependence of Matthew upon Mark. It is especially in studying the parallel passages that one comes to see the plausibility of such a hypothesis. For example, it would be hard to explain why Mark would have a much more negative attitude towards Jesus' brothers and possibly Mary if he were dependent on Matthew who definitely does not appear as negative towards Mary and who is also more lenient towards the disciples of Jesus than is Mark. Let us now look at the passages:

Matthew 12:46-50	Mark 3:31-35
[46] While he was still speaking to the people, behold, his mother and his brothers stood outside, asking to speak to him. [47] Someone told him, "Look, your mother and your brothers are standing outside, wanting to speak to you." [48] But he replied to the man who told him, "Who is my mother, and who are my brothers?" [49] And stretching out his hand toward his disciples, he said, "Here are my mother and my brothers! [50] For whoever does the will of my Father in heaven is my brother, and sister, and mother."	[31] And his mother and his brothers came; and standing outside they sent word to him and called him. [32] And a crowd was sitting about him and they said to him "Your mother and your brothers are outside, asking for you." [33] And he replied, "Who are my mother and my brothers?" [34] And looking around on those who sat about him, he said, "Here are my mother and my brothers! [35] Whoever does the will of God is my brother, and sister, and mother."

In Matthew we see relatively little interest in the fact of Jesus' mother and brothers coming to see him. Moreover, verse 47 is missing from earlier manuscripts and seems to be an added feature from conflating Luke and Mark later in the tradition of manuscripts. In Matthew there is no disavowal of the family as such; rather Jesus' relationship to the Father in heaven (Matthew uses the more Jewish expression) is what is important for all who would follow and listen to Jesus. Notice also that Matthew precisely identifies those who are near Jesus as "disciples," that is, those who immediately followed Jesus and the Christian believers of Matthew's time. Mark does not call them disciples. There is also the gesture of Jesus stretching his hand over his disciples as if to commission and bless them. This is not present in Mark. Frank W. Beare comments, "Both Matthew and Luke have omitted the reference to the hostility of the family, and in their versions the words of Jesus are taken as conferring on his followers the high honor of recognition as members of his family" (F. W. Beare, *The Earliest Records of Jesus*, p. 104). Even more to the point, J. L. McKenzie states, "The new unity Jesus forms about himself is a unity in which other bonds, even the bonds of kinship, are sublimated. Jesus does not reject the bonds of kinship, but raises all who believe in him to an intimacy of kinship. His own kin exclude themselves from this new unity if they do not believe in him. Again in fairness to the kinsmen, the saying does not imply that they do not believe in Jesus" (*JBC*, Matthew 43:87, p. 86).

Actually, Matthew is not giving us any information that we do not already possess in Mark. In fact, most exegetes believe that he is dependent on Mark and merely adapts the pericope to his own theological intention as well as the ordering of his Gospel narrative. He trims away any of the negative elements that may be present in Mark's account. There is no further insight either into the situation of whether Mary had other children or not. The term brother or sister is understood as related to Jesus. In fact, the New Testament knows nothing of any children of Joseph and Mary nor do the earliest traditions after the New Testament. It is true that the doctrine of the perpetual virginity of Mary influences most Catholic exegetes to see the notion of relatives implied in the "brothers and sisters." Joseph Blinzler's book is still the classic work on this question. His conclusion is that these are "cousins" of Jesus, not offspring of Mary and Joseph nor of Joseph from a former marriage.

The final parallel passage between Matthew and Mark is the account of Jesus being rejected at Nazareth. Here are the parallels:

Mark 6:1-6	Matthew 13:54-58
He left that place and came to his hometown, and his disciples followed him. ²On the Sabbath he began to teach in the synagogue, and many who heard him were astounded. They said, "Where did this man get all this? What is this wisdom that has been given to him? What deeds of power are being done by his hands! ³Is not this the carpenter, the son of Mary and brother of James and Joses and Judas and Simon, and are not his sisters here with us?" And they took offense at him. ⁴Then Jesus said to them, "Prophets are not without honor, except in their hometown, and among their own kin, and in their own house." ⁵And he could do no deed of power there, except that he laid his hands on a few sick people and cured them. ⁶And he was amazed at their unbelief.	⁵⁴He came to his hometown and began to teach the people in their synagogue, so that they were astounded and said, "Where did this man get this wisdom and these deeds of power? ⁵⁵Is not this the carpenter's son? Is not his mother called Mary? And are not his brothers James and Joseph and Simon and Judas? ⁵⁶And are not all his sisters with us? Where then did this man get all this?" ⁵⁷And they took offense at him. But Jesus said to them, "Prophets are not without honor except in their own country and in their own house." ⁵⁸And he did not do many deeds of power there, because of their unbelief.

Both Mark and Matthew are bringing to a close Jesus' ministry in Galilee with this passage. On this point they are in agreement. Matthew, however, revises and omits certain expressions of Mark. Jesus is not called the carpenter as in Mark but the son of the carpenter. What is significant is that neither Mark nor Matthew call Jesus the son of Joseph here. In this passage, Matthew does not harken back to what he indicated in the genealogy and the narrative of the birth story, hence, he is faithfully transmitting a separate tradition which he has borrowed from Mark's Gospel. Jesus normally would have been called *bar-Joseph* if he were the carnal son of Joseph. In the last of the Gospel traditions, that of the Fourth

Evangelist, the people who think they know Jesus' origins state: "Is this not Jesus, the son of Joseph, whose father and mother we know? How does he say, 'I have come down from heaven'?" (Jn 6:42). Matthew omits the emotional response that Jesus was amazed at their unbelief; he also shows Jesus deliberately not performing many miracles there; not, as Mark says, that he could not perform them.

Conclusion

In Matthew's Gospel the image of Mary has become clearer even though we are farther from the time of the historical Mary of Nazareth. It seems to be a principle of biblical writings that traditions are given more detail as time passes on. The biblical language is also the language of a community of believers who have been receivers of authentic testimony on the part of the eye-witnesses as well as the authors of sacred books. Matthew, who represents the third generation of Jewish-Christian believers has continued the tradition of remembering what Jesus did and taught. His narrative answers the questions and the needs of his own community which faced the tension of a schism, for it can be described as a community which is in danger of dividing against itself. Some would return to Pharisaic Judaism which now is flourishing and is to continue with its great interest and dedication in the revealed Word of God in the Hebrew Scriptures. On the other hand, both Jews and Gentiles who had heard about Jesus were now coming in greater numbers and presented new problems of a cultural as well as an ethical nature. Matthew's task is to deepen the instruction of the community in such a way that both would be strengthened and united through the message of the Good News. From the facts that follow, we can be assured that Matthew's Gospel achieved its purpose and also became one of the most cherished liturgical Gospels in the history of the Church and it continues to be so.

Matthew went beyond the simple Jewish background of Paul's

description of the woman who gave Jesus life. He also surpassed the abrupt and even disconcerting image of Mary that Mark offered. Matthew's image is that of the Mother of the Messiah who is also a virgin espoused to Joseph of the house of David. She brings to a conclusion the long expectation for a Davidic Messiah as is seen in Matthew's use of Isaiah 7:14, but more than that, she embraces the non-Jewish members of the community to whom Matthew speaks his Gospel for she is also a daughter in the line of Abraham her ancestor in faith. She is virgin in chapter one; mother in chapter two. She is Jewish in the lineage of Jesus and Davidic through the reverence and acceptance Joseph has for her and the child to be born. She represents a promise to the Gentiles or the Nations because she, too, like Abraham is among those who believe in God's promise of salvation.

By using the genealogies of the Hebrew Scriptures, Matthew demonstrates how Jesus is truly the descendant of David through Joseph and thus, for the Jewish-Christian believers, is the Messiah. His profound presentation of Isaiah 7:14 — "Behold a virgin shall conceive and bring forth a son and they shall call him Emmanuel" underlines the birth and genesis of Jesus as son of David. Through the power of the Holy Spirit the child is also a son of Abraham, and Mary is the link for this paradox. Yes, Matthew has completed what Paul began in his letters, namely, the Jewishness of Jesus and his mother Mary. All that Paul hinted at and all that Mark recorded is now taken up by Matthew in a developed biblical tradition.

Matthew presents Jesus as the fulfillment of what the evangelist understood to be the purpose of the Hebrew Scriptures. He uses fulfillment formulas and texts more often than all the other evangelists. His special emphasis on Jesus as Messiah continues not only in the birth narrative but also in the ministry of Jesus and in the Paschal Mysteries. Matthew thus has prepared us for the next stage of Christological and Marian development. He has spoken reverently of the Mother of the Messiah. He sets the stage for Luke who will allow the virgin to speak for herself.

Endnotes

1. Jack D. Kingsbury, *Matthew: Structure, Christology, Kingdom* (Philadelphia: Fortress, 1975), pp. 7-17.
2. M.D. Johnson, *The Purpose of the Biblical Genealogies with Special Reference to the Setting of the Genealogies of Jesus* (*NTSMS* 8; Cambridge University, 1969).

Chapter Four

LUKE'S PORTRAIT OF
MARY, THE MOTHER OF JESUS

Luke's Gospel is usually dated around 85 C.E. This would indicate that his Good News is addressed to Christians of the third generation after the death of Jesus. Luke today is most often studied with its sequel, the Acts of the Apostles, which takes up the narrative about the first followers who continue the work and words of Jesus in the communities which are being called into being as "Church." Luke is most probably a Gentile convert who had studied the Jewish Scriptures very carefully. He came to know about Jesus of Nazareth at Antioch in Syria where he tells us the term "Christian" was used for the first time (Ac 11:25). Luke's use of Koine Greek is superior to that of the other evangelists. He transposes it from the highest literary style and vocabulary (Lk 1:1-4) to the Septuagintal use in his narrative about John the Baptist (Lk 1:5-25), to simple narrative Greek in the Acts of the Apostles.

In recent years, efforts have been made to study the third evangelist in his composite work Luke-Acts.[1] This shows the continuity of Jesus' message in the story of the followers of Jesus who continue his mission and message in the churches which are formed first in Judea, then Samaria, then throughout the Mediterranean. In our study of Mary, we will see that there is an important reference to her in the Acts of the Apostles. It is the last time she appears in the New Testament after the death of Jesus (Ac 1:14).[2]

With our opening of the pages of Luke, we enter into a more developed image of Mary which brings her closer to the communities influenced by this excellent Gospel. Luke, the evangelist, enables Mary to speak for herself and gives us enough information about her to form a definite portrait. It is from Luke's Gospel that authentic knowledge of Mary and devotion to her emanates. The dogma and doctrine that develop around her in the ensuing centuries can be likened to the rabbinic development around the Torah, acting as a hedge to protect as well as present the mysteries of God and the Spirit in her life, words, and actions.

It is primarily in the Infancy Narrative of Luke (1:5-2:52) that we find material which directly focuses upon Mary for the first time as a person. We have seen from Matthew's Infancy Narrative that this inspirational form of the Gospels is a complex body of narrative that is at times based on history, traditions, and fulfillment and is grounded on events as well as on symbolic understanding of these events in the history of salvation. Once again, like Matthew's Infancy Narrative, Luke's too will present an even richer Christology, a more tempered use of the Hebrew Scriptures for fulfillment of prophecy, and some special theological insights not found elsewhere in the Gospels. Like the other inspired evangelists, Luke is both theologian and author.

Great credit has to be given to Father Raymond E. Brown for his monumental work on *The Birth of the Messiah*.[3] This commentary on both Matthew and Luke's Infancy Narratives helps us to establish a sound foundation for the rest of our Mariological research. Brown has been followed by Joseph Fitzmyer's commentary on Luke in the Anchor Bible which also gives us further exegesis on the Marian passages.[4] Prior to this Fr. René Laurentin's work on the structure of the first two chapters of Luke set the stage for modern exegetical study of Mary.[5]

The Annunciation Account: Luke 1:26-38

[26]In the sixth month the angel Gabriel was sent by God to a town in Galilee called Nazareth,

[27]to a virgin engaged to a man whose name was Joseph, of
the house of David. The virgin's name was Mary.
[28]And he came to her and said, "Greetings, favored one! The
Lord is with you."
[29]But she was much perplexed by his words and pondered
what sort of greeting this might be.
[30]The angel said to her, "Do not be afraid, Mary, for you
have found favor with God.
[31]And now, you will conceive in your womb and bear a son,
and you will name him Jesus.
[32]He will be great, and will be called the Son of the Most
High, and the Lord God will give to him the throne
of his ancestor David.
[33]He will reign over the house of Jacob forever, and of his
kingdom there will be no end."
[34]Mary said to the angel, "How can this be since I am a
virgin?"
[35]The angel said to her, "The Holy Spirit will come upon
you, and the power of the Most High will overshadow
you; therefore the child to be born will be holy; he
will be called Son of God.
[36]And now, your relative Elizabeth in her old age has also
conceived a son; and this is the sixth month for her
who is said to be barren.
[37]For nothing will be impossible with God."
[38]Then Mary said, "Here am I, the servant of the Lord; let it
be with me according to your word." Then the angel
departed from her.

Luke starts at the beginning as he gives us the earliest depic-
tion of Mary in her personal life as a maiden of twelve or thirteen
years of age. He writes from the perspective of Resurrection faith,
touching upon Mary in terms of the mystery of her own calling to
be the Virgin Mother of the Holy One, Jesus.

He has carefully prepared us for this Annunciation to Mary by
what has preceded in the narrative about the foretelling of the birth
of John the Baptist. That birth narrative is also presented through an
annunciation to Zechariah. Luke is helping us through such a

diptych or parallel to interpret the meaning of Mary's call. There are clues within his writing that show how Luke connects the two accounts: the mention of the sixth month of the pregnancy of Elizabeth and the same messenger of God, Gabriel. Then the contrasts of Zechariah in the south, the temple in Jerusalem with Mary in the north, Nazareth in Galilee; and Elizabeth's advanced age and barrenness with Mary's youth and potential. Zechariah and Elizabeth are from the priestly family of Aaron; the spouse of Mary, Joseph, is of the house of David.

Luke also makes use of a literary form called an "Annunciation." It is a form which has appeared many times in the Hebrew Scriptures and also in the Gospel of Matthew. It is helpful to look at it in the light of form criticism. We can compare Luke's Annunciation with that of Matthew. Raymond E. Brown's schema seems to be the best since he gathers the biblical references to other annunciations including the two from Luke, that of John the Baptist and Mary. I would also suggest that we add the call of Jeremiah and Isaiah to these references since they complement a call to holiness. Jeremiah shows that his call occurs even prior to his birth. There are five steps in these annunciation patterns:

1. The *appearance* of an angel of the Lord (or an appearance of the Lord)
2. *Fear* or prostration of the visionary confronted by the supernatural presence
3. The divine *message:*
   a. The visionary is addressed by name
   b. A qualifying phrase describing the visionary
   c. The visionary is urged not to be afraid
   d. A woman is with child or is about to be with child
   e. She will give birth to the (male) child
   f. The name by which the child is to be called
   g. An etymology interpreting the name
   h. The future accomplishments of the child
4. An *objection* by the visionary as to how this can be or a request for a sign
5. The *giving of a sign* to reassure the visionary

(The biblical references for "Annunciation Patterns" are given by R.E. Brown in *The Birth of the Messiah*, pp. 155-158.)

Ignace de la Potterie has studied the Annunciation to Mary and given us the following structural analysis in his book *Mary in the Mystery of the Covenant*:[6]

26-27	Introduction		Mission of Angel Gabriel
	A Salutation	THE ANGEL	
	(a)		"Rejoice! in having been FOUND FULL OF GRACE
	(b)		the Lord is WITH YOU
I 28-29	B Consternation	MARY	At this word she was very troubled
	A' Announcement	THE ANGEL	
	(1)	(a')	...You have found GRACE before God AND BEHOLD: you are going *to conceive and bring forth a son* and you will give him the name Jesus. And he will be great and will be called SON OF THE MOST HIGH.
II 30-34	B' Difficulty	MARY	How will this be done since I have never known man? (since I am a VIRGIN)?
III 35-38b	A" Announcement (2)	THE ANGEL (b')	The Holy Spirit will come UPON YOU And the power of the Most High will take you under his shadow. That is why he who will be born holy will be called SON OF GOD.
	(SIGN)		AND BEHOLD: Elizabeth . . . she, also, has *conceived a son* she who is called BARREN.

B" Consent	MARY
	BEHOLD the handmaid of the Lord may it happen to me according to his word.

38c	Conclusion	And the angel left her.

Both from the Annunciation schema and from the structured format of de la Potterie, we see that the narrative is a unit within Luke's Gospel of salvation history. Luke, as we have noted, knits the narrative to the preceding one (Lk 1:5-25) and also to what follows in the Visitation pericope. Both Zechariah and Elizabeth are involved in what precedes and what follows the Annunciation to Mary. Even within the same pericope Luke makes use of inclusions; for example, the virgin whose name is Mary in Luke 1:27 is responding from that status as virgin in verse 34: "Since I do not know man" or more accurately as the *New Revised Standard Version* says "since I am a virgin." (So, too, the translation of de la Potterie as we see in the structured presentation.)

The same divine messenger, Gabriel, whose name means the "Strength of God" or "Man of God," is also a link to what has preceded. He is the harbinger of the Good News both to the parents of the precursor, John the Baptist, and the holy one, the Son of God, Jesus. Gabriel shows us that mediation is common both to the Hebrew Scriptures and the Christian Gospels. Both angels and humans are involved in the salvific plan of God. We can also see this in the schema of the Annunciations from the Hebrew Scriptures and in the mediation of Abraham, Jacob, and Moses who dialogue and make a covenant with the living God. It is no different for Mary as she enters into dialogue with Gabriel.

Verse 26 picks up the time-line of Elizabeth's pregnancy: "it was in the sixth month" that Gabriel now appears to Mary. Verse 36 has another inclusion: "for the one who is called barren is in her sixth month." Verse 56 points out that the visit of Mary lasts until the term of her cousin is finished: "And Mary remained with her three months."

Verse 27: Here Luke unlike Matthew centers exclusively on the virgin Mary rather than on Joseph who is of the house of David. Twice within this verse the term "virgin" is used (*parthenos*). The name of Mary follows. It is she who is fully awake and who listens to Gabriel. We are not told that she is of the house of David even though several earlier theologians like John Chrysostom cleverly argue from the grammar that she is. Rather she would be, like her cousins Elizabeth and Zechariah, of the priestly line of Aaron or of the Levitical lineage. Modern exegetes and grammarians point out that the antecedent pronoun refers to Joseph, not to Mary.

Verse 28 is God's first greeting to Mary through Gabriel. The expression, "You have been found to be full of grace," is important for knowing who Mary is in the plan of salvation and how she is called or named by God. In the Greek the term *kecharitomene* is a perfect passive participle which means that Mary already is found to be with grace even before she gives her consent to be the mother of the Messiah. Ignace de la Potterie has carefully traced the use of this expression in the Scriptures and in Greek literature; he also has shown its theological significance (See "Kecharitomene en Lc 1,28. Étude philologique," *Biblica* 68 (1987), pp. 357-382; "Kecharitomene en Lc 1,28. Étude exégétique et théologique," *Biblica* 69 (1988), pp. 480-508; and *Mary in the Mystery of the Covenant*, pp. 17-20).

As early as 1957 this term was studied in the interpretation of the Fathers of the Church and through the medieval scholars by F. Marchisano, but it is through the insightful studies of de la Potterie that we see this expression as indicative of the complete holiness of Mary at the time of her calling. The Vulgate's translation *plena gratiae* that is, full of grace, is not rigorously exact (cf. Ac 6:8 where Stephen is said to be "full of grace").

The verb from which this appellation of Mary is derived is rarely used in the New Testament. Only here and in Ephesians 1:6 (which incidentally is used in *Redemptoris Mater* by John Paul II) do we find it, however in different verbal forms. The verb belongs to a class called causative verbs, that is, verbs which indicate what is brought about, what happens or is caused in the recipient or subject. Our verse indicates that there has already been a transformation caused by grace in the person of Mary. Thus it looks to her present condition as the virgin of Nazareth already found to be with the grace of God in an abundant way. With such an accurate translation and interpretation we can see within the earliest traditions of the Church why Mary is considered to be the all-holy one. This is the earliest moment spoken about Mary in the Scriptures. She would be within her twelfth or thirteenth year, for that was the customary age to be betrothed to her spouse Joseph. Origen and Ambrose point out that in the entire Bible only Mary is called *kecharitomene*. In the other text of Ephesians 1:6, John Chrysostom translates it in reference to the universal call to holiness: "God has transformed us with this marvelous grace" (*PG* 62:13-14).

Brown and Fitzmyer apply this holiness to Mary in light of the birth of the Messiah or Mary's divine maternity, but the text itself does not refer yet to the birth of the child, hence, Mary as virgin and not as mother is already confirmed in God's favor or grace. Chronologically, literally, and theologically this text can be seen as referring then to the holiness of Mary prior to the birth of Jesus. The transformation of Mary operated by the grace of God has already taken place prior to the Annunciation. Sophronius of Jerusalem states: "No one has been fully sanctified as you have . . . no one has been purified in advance as you have" (*PG* 87/3, 3248).

Our text then is the one that is helpful in understanding from the Scriptures the dogma of the Immaculate Conception. It is not a "proof text," but a text that has traditionally been used to understand Mary's holiness. Exegesis does not have as its task to demonstrate or to prove dogma, but if we keep in mind what has just been said we are better prepared to see how there is a development of dogma because of the tradition based on certain texts of the Scripture. The tension and dialogue between text and event is not only an historical-critical process, but also a profound reflection on the truths of salvation as they come to us through the teaching and the tradition of the Church. Evidently, we do not have in Luke a statement about

Mary being preserved from sin from the first moment of her conception or existence.

But what in reality does the text say and what does the dogma mean? That God in his loving kindness has graced Mary, that is, she is in no way turned away from God. This is precisely the biblical notion of grace. Grace takes away all sin (cf. Ep 1:6-7). If then, Mary was totally transformed by the grace of God, this includes God's preserving her from sin, for God has purified and sanctified her already. We can see how rich the text is for such "mysteries" in the life of this specially chosen one. Her virginity, her holiness, her divine maternity, and the symbolism of the Daughter of Zion are implied.

In verse 29 we see the consternation of Mary: she is troubled or perplexed by these words of Gabriel. She inquires of the angel about such a calling or naming. Immediately, in the response given by the angel in verse 30 there is an inclusion to what the angel has already said, that is, a parallel explanation to her being called *kecharitomene*. Gabriel tells Mary "you have found favor with God." The angel also uses the present imperative, telling Mary to cease from this moment being afraid.

In verses 31 and 32 we have Luke's more subtle way of showing fulfillment of a promise made in the Scriptures. Luke does not use a direct citation of Isaiah 7:14 as Matthew had done, but rather implies it. The birth of Jesus is foretold in this Lucan Annunciation in the light of the Emmanuel passage (compare Lk 1:31 with Mt 1:23 [Is 7:14]). Luke in a subtle way uses the thought of the text so that it fits into the actual calling of Mary to respond in trust and faith to the angel and to the event of conceiving and giving birth to Jesus. We, as believers, already know the full story of Jesus' life and his Paschal Mystery so we are not surprised at Gabriel speaking of Jesus even before he is conceived. Luke is painting this scene within the leisure of his own contemplative reflection, capturing it through a *kairos* lens rather than through a precise chronological moment. The leisure of *kairos* envisions the entire mystery of Christ at a glance through Resurrection faith.

It helps us to understand Luke better if we keep in mind the great skill he uses in weaving themes throughout his Gospel and Acts while showing continuity amidst discontinuity (as we have seen in Zechariah and Mary). In his most recent commentary on the Resurrection appearances, Fr. Robert Karris shows us these themes as already present in the initial chapters of Luke, that is, in the Infancy Narrative. Of the Emmaus account he says, "This exquisite story, found only in this Gospel, sparkles with Lucan themes, especially those of journey, faith as seeing, and hospitality" (*NJBC* 43:196, p. 720). Continuing along the same line of thought, Karris concludes his commentary on Luke 24:50-53 with the following statement: "These verses contain numerous cross references to 1:5-2:52 as Luke rounds off his themes via inclusion" (*NJBC* 43:198, p. 721).

Verses 32 and 33. The titles of Christ appear: "He will be great, and will be called the Son of the Most High, and the Lord God will give him the throne of his ancestor David. He will reign over the house of Jacob forever, and of his kingdom there will be no end." These titles affirm the Messianic and Christological names that will be applied to Jesus throughout Luke's Gospel. Exegetes state this is Luke's post-Resurrection Christology which is being placed into the Infancy Narrative. Thus it occurs a stage earlier than in Mark's Gospel. It remains for John to complete the scope of New Testament Christology. He affirms the pre-existence of the Word which then becomes incarnate (Jn 1:1, 14). Certainly Luke's titles lean toward an ascending Christology and point towards the divinity of Jesus. There is in Luke, however, no hint of the eternal nature of the child nor is he called "Logos" or "Word." Luke's titles are taken from the Davidic and Messianic covenantal promises of a faithful God. All spring from the maternal waters of the Hebrew Scriptures. Mary, too, is seen within the context of Judaism and its prophetic heritage.

Verse 34 shows us Mary asking how all this is possible since she has had no marital relationship with Joseph.

Verse 35 opens up the dialogue through the angel's response

that the Holy Spirit, that is, the power of God, will overshadow her and thus the one born will be called holy and a son of God.

Charles Talbert comments: "Verse 35 indicates how this will come to pass: he will be conceived of the Holy Spirit. It is because of his conception by the Holy Spirit that Jesus is Son of God (note the "therefore"). Since Son of God is used for Adam in 3:38, and for the Risen Christ in Acts 13:13, this title in Luke-Acts may be employed for one who lives because of God's direct, creative intervention. . . . With Matthew, Luke speaks only of Mary's *virginitas ante partum* (virginity before giving birth; i.e., she conceived Jesus without the involvement of a man): Jesus was miraculously conceived by the Holy Sp rit (1:35). It is by virtue of this miraculous conception in the womb of the virgin Mary that Jesus is the Son of God" (C. H. Talbert, *Reading Luke — A Literary and Theological Commentary on the Third Gospel*, Crossroad, New York, 1982, p. 19).

Verse 36 takes us from the realm of mystery — God's plan — to the reality of the present. Elizabeth, Mary's cousin, is already in her sixth month. Verse 37 confirms this, "for nothing will be impossible with God."

Verse 38 completes the dialogue with Mary's response. It is a free consent to the summons of God, to God's call. Luke concludes the Annunciation narrative with masterful artistry: "'Here I am, the servant of the Lord; let it be with me according to your word.' Then the angel departed from her."

Mary visits Elizabeth: Luke 1:39-45

> [39]In those days Mary set out and went with haste to a Judean town in the hill country,
> [40]where she entered the house of Zechariah and greeted Elizabeth.
> [41]When Elizabeth heard Mary's greeting, the child leaped in her womb. And Elizabeth was filled with the Holy Spirit

[42]and exclaimed with a loud cry, "Blessed are you among
    women, and blessed is the fruit of your womb.
[43]And why has this happened to me, that the mother of my
    Lord comes to me?
[44]For as soon as I heard the sound of your greeting, the child
    in my womb leaped for joy.
[45]And blessed is she who believed that there would be a
    fulfillment of what was spoken to her by the Lord."

This pericope is commonly called the Visitation for it contains
the meeting of two believing women who, by confiding in the word
of God, now share the grace of being pregnant with two children
who will have special missions in God's saving plan. The eagerness
or haste of Mary and the loud cry of Elizabeth praising Mary shows
the exuberant joy of these expectant mothers. Luke fashions this
narrative in the pattern of the surprise of Sarah in her giving birth
to Isaac and in the stirring of Jacob and Esau within the womb of
Rebekah (Gn 18:14ff. and Gn 25:22ff.). C. Stuhlmueller comments:
"This action of Elizabeth's unborn child not only reminds us of
Rebekah's children (Gn 25:22ff.) and David's dance before the Ark
(2 S 6:16) but also of the messianic leap of joy among the poor (Is
35:6; Ps 114:6; Ml 3:20)" (*JBC* 44:35, p. 123).

The passage also serves as a link to what has preceded both in
the canticle of Zechariah and what follows in the Magnificat of
Mary. It also unites the triad of Elizabeth, Zechariah, and John the
Baptist with that of Mary, Joseph, and Jesus. The fulfillment of the
first covenant flows into the second covenant at the advent of the
Messiah.

Mary is depicted throughout this pericope as the model
believer (see Lk 1:38) and it is Elizabeth who proclaims her blessed
because she has believed (verse 42 and 45). Joseph Fitzmyer tells us,
"The beatitude in v. 45 serves to foreshadow the beatitude that will
be expressed over Mary by the woman in the crowd in 11:27-28:
here Mary's faith is explicitly mentioned; in 11:28 the second
beatitude, Jesus' reply to the woman, implies Mary's hearing the

word of God and keeping it [cf. 8:21]" (J. Fitzmyer, *Luke: Anchor Bible*, Vol. 28, p. 358).

The Visitation is thus the point of departure for Mary's active journey of faith. This will alert the reader to the journey narrative of Jesus himself (Lk 9:51-19:48) where Jesus carefully prepares his own disciples for entering into the mystery of his Exodus to God. Jesus makes this initial journey with his mother and through the meeting of Mary and Elizabeth prepares in joy the mission of his own precursor, John the Baptist.

Elizabeth's expression, "And why has this happened to me that the mother of my Lord comes to me?" refers to Mary and her child Jesus. Jesus is called Lord. Luke will return to this title in the Gospel (Lk 20:41-44) and in Acts (2:34) where a citation of Psalm 110 is used, "The Lord said to my Lord, sit at my right hand." Though exegetes carefully refrain from stating definitively that this makes Jesus the equal of God, the Church's tradition proclaims both the divine maternity and the divinity of Jesus in the light of this text. This verse is the one that comes closest to the title *Theotokos* for Mary, that is, God-bearer. That "Lord" means God is confirmed by every use of the term thus far in the Gospel of Luke. Mary's Magnificat will immediately use the same word for God.

As to the title "Blessed Virgin" or "Blessed Mother," we see that it is a direct use of the words of Elizabeth's praise of Mary. Mary will be declared blessed more than once in this Gospel. She is the beatitudes personified. She is a joyful, happy, fortunate, and blessed woman of faith. Luke probably was aware of a similar expression in the Hebrew Scriptures where Jael is called blessed among women in Judges 5:24 and where Judith is addressed in Judith 13:18: "O daughter, you are blessed by the Most High God above all other women on earth." The Canticle in 1:8 speaks of the loved one in similar terms, "O fairest among women."

Mary may have first made this journey of faith within her own heart. We read that she journeys to Elizabeth with great eagerness or great haste (*meta spoudes*). Later she ponders over the events and words of God (Lk 2:19, 51). The actual journey from Nazareth to

the home of Zechariah would be seventy to eighty miles in length.
It may have taken her a full week to cover the distance to Ain Karem
to the southwest of Jerusalem. Today this little village is nestled in
a valley surrounded by the gentle sloping mountains of Judea. It is
not far from the road through the desert which leads east to the
Dead Sea and the area of the community of Qumran. In Ain Karem
is a convent with a church surrounded by a garden. On the walls are
beautiful panels of the Magnificat in about two dozen languages.
The scene is tranquil and refreshing and must have been so for Mary,
too. Today it is a place of prayer and retreat.

The Magnificat: Mary's Song of Joy and Praise of Yahweh

[46]And Mary said,
[47]"My soul magnifies the Lord, and my spirit rejoices in God
     my Savior,
[48]for he has looked with favor on the lowliness (*tapeinosen*) of
     his servant.
  Surely, from now on all generations will call me blessed;
[49]for the Mighty One has done great things for me, and holy
     is his name.
[50]His mercy is for those who fear him from generation to
     generation.
[51]He has shown strength with his arm; he has scattered the
     proud in the thoughts of their hearts.
[52]He has brought down the powerful from their thrones, and
     lifted up the lowly (*tapeinous*).
[53]He has filled the hungry with good things, and sent the
     rich away empty.
[54]He has helped his servant Israel, in remembrance of his
     mercy,
[55]according to the promise he made to our ancestors, to
     Abraham and to his descendants forever."
[56]And Mary remained with her about three months and then
     returned to her home.

The Magnificat of Mary continues a refrain in hymnody of what has happened to Mary both in the Annunciation and in the Visitation. This is Mary's hymn of praise to God for the wonders that are being accomplished. A few scholars choose to attribute the Magnificat to Elizabeth because of some important early manuscripts and witnesses (like Irenaeus, Origen, and Nicetas). The Lucan themes that have just been indicated in the scene of the meeting of the two women believers, Mary and Elizabeth, continue: joy, Mary's humble acknowledgment of the blessings bestowed on her by Elizabeth, the lowliness of God's servant (*tapencsis*), and the fulfillment of God's promises made to Abraham.

Luke sets this hymn after a very simple introduction attested to by all the Greek manuscripts: "And Mary said" and concludes it in verse 56 by bringing the meeting and visit to an end. Mary is center-stage and has been since the Annunciation. Luke, however, is the composer of the hymn as we now have it. In it Mary continues to speak using Luke's theological and evangelical language. Has Luke taken this hymn from an ancient Jewish one? Was it a hymn first addressed in the Baptist's circle? Are these the words of Mary herself? Is it an early Jewish-Christian hymn similar to those found at Qumran (the *Hodayot*) but replete with Christian perspectives? These are the questions about its source and composition that every scholar wrestles with as the Magnificat continues to be studied and reflected upon.[7]

The Magnificat is Mary's response to God as well as her acknowledgment of Elizabeth's praise of her as being blessed among all women. If we carefully look at what Elizabeth has said of Mary in 1:42, 43, 45 and at the expressions of joy and exuberance that both women display in this supportive and courageous meeting, we discover that Mary's hymn is a continuous response to the events that have just happened. There are also many implicit allusions from almost the whole of the Hebrew Scriptures (and Luke likes to use the Torah, the Prophets, and the Writings; see Lk 24:25, 44).

There is also the technique of parallelism both synthetic and antithetical, so characteristic of the Psalms, within Luke's composition of the Magnificat. He matches the Annunciation accounts and now does the same, with Zechariah's Benedictus being followed by Mary's Magnificat. The balance of a man with a woman or an image that is masculine with one that is feminine is also present and will continue throughout Luke-Acts. The Magnificat also elicits the following biblical themes which are characteristically Lucan: joy, fulfillment of God's promises, the reversal of the mighty by the lowly, the merciful love of God for the people Israel, the praise of Yahweh by servants like Mary and Elizabeth, the *macarism* or blessings of Mary, the conversion of minds and hearts and salvation.

Using the genre of a hymn of praise we discover that the canticle of Mary is similar in structure to Psalms 33, 47, 48, 113, 117, 135, and 136. These psalms contain (1) an introductory invitation to praise God, (2) then a body giving the reasons why God should be praised, and (3) a conclusion which repeats the elements of the body. Using R.E. Brown's masterful analysis of the hymn, we also can say that the following biblical references are implied in the Magnificat: Ps 35:9; 1 S 2:1-2; Hab 3:18; 1 S 1:11; Gn 29:32; Gn 30:13; Dt 10:21; Zp 3:17; Ps 111:9; Ps 103:17; 1 S 2:7-8; Ps 89:11; Si 10:14; Jb 12:19; Ezk 21:31 (26); Ps 107:9; Is 41:8-9; and Ps 98:3. In addition to the biblical references there are the following: IV Ezra 9:45; Psalms of Solomon 13:11; 1 QM xiv: 10-11.

The Magnificat together with the Benedictus is more Semitic in style than the rest of the narrative in Luke's Infancy Narrative. It seems to spring from a primitive Jewish-Christian community that is overwhelmed by the salvation of God coming to Israel in a new way. The *anawim* or the lowly ones who believed and understood this salvation were probably those who used this hymn originally. They would identify themselves as totally dependent on God; the "remnant of Israel" that now is experiencing the benefits of salvation from a merciful, loving God. R.E. Brown says, "it is not impossible that, in the last third of the century when he was composing Luke-Acts, Luke came upon these canticles in a Greek-speaking Jewish Christian community in an area influenced by Jerusalem Christianity" (*Birth of the Messiah*, 355).

The Birth of Jesus: Luke 2:1-7

[1]In those days a decree went out from Caesar Augustus that all the world should be registered.
[2]This was the first registration and was taken while Quirinius was governor of Syria.
[3]All went to their own towns to be registered.
[4]Joseph also went from the town of Nazareth in Galilee to Judea, to the city of David called Bethlehem, because he was descended from the house and family of David.
[5]He went to be registered with Mary, to whom he was engaged and who was expecting a child.
[6]While they were there, the time came for her to deliver her child.
[7]And she gave birth to her firstborn son and wrapped him in bands of cloth, and laid him in a manger, because there was no place for him in the inn.

Luke's narrative of the birth of Jesus is the most descriptive one in the New Testament. Matthew gives us more of a scriptural reflection upon it based on Isaiah 7:14, but Luke who is writing to a Gentile audience places the nativity within the context of world history as he knows it. This is also another indication of Luke's universalism which will continue in the Gospel and in Acts. Mary is central throughout chapter two, but there are some notable differences from what we learned in Luke's initial chapter.

The remainder of the Infancy Narrative in Luke seems to have been written independently from what was recorded in chapter one, for Joseph now appears side by side with Mary as a mutual cooperating partner in the plan of salvation. Mary again is reintroduced as his betrothed and Joseph's relationship to the house and family of David is mentioned anew. No mention is made of the virginal conception. Luke may be directly responsible for 2:1-5; for the rest of chapter two he seems to be depending on a source. Hence, the inaccuracies of the census of Quirinius probably stem from Luke rather than from his source. Nor are they to be attributed to Mary, especially when it comes to the discrepancies found in Luke concerning the law of purification of the mother in Leviticus. Most likely, Luke is composing his own theological perceptions and description of the birth of Jesus in the light of Old Testament themes and stories.

In chapter one, Luke places the reader in the atmosphere of Judaism and the Hebrew Scriptures. Now, in chapter two, with the birth of Jesus we are in the context of world history, for Luke turns to the Gentile world for setting the stage of Jesus' birth. A new era is beginning after that of John the Baptist and that of his parents, Elizabeth and Zechariah. Luke wishes the "good news" of Jesus' birth to be proclaimed and known throughout the whole world of the Roman Empire. Thus the enrollment in a census under Caesar Augustus while Quirinius was legate in Syria is the historical datum that Luke offers the reader to show that Jesus is also a light of revelation to the Gentiles as well as the glory of his people Israel (Lk 2:32). Luke's universalism is central even in his Infancy Narrative.

The famous problem of such a census under Quirinius who was legate only in 6 C.E. contradicts Luke's information (see Josephus, *Antiquities* XVII, 13, 5; XVIII, 1, 1). Luke seems to refer to this same census in Acts 5:37 evidently in connection with the revolt of Judas the Galilean during the time of Herod the Great (who died in 4 B.C.E.). G.W.H. Lampe capsules the point in noting, "A census ordered by Augustus could scarcely have taken place in Herod's dominions without provoking disturbances, and would be unlikely to be unnoticed by Josephus. Luke's allusion to this as the 'first enrollment' suggests that he is thinking of the census which, as the first to be held under the Roman administration of Judaea, caused the revolt of Judas of Galilee" (*Peake's Commentary on the Bible*, "Luke," by G.W.H. Lampe, p. 825). Rather than defend Luke's historical accuracy, it is more appropriate to see the theological intention he had in placing Jesus' birth in such a context of history which would be the appointed time for salvation history in the birth of the Messiah. Luke is already looking to his goal, the bringing of this

Good News even to Rome, the capital of the Empire. Within chapter two, many of the Lucan themes of Luke-Acts appear: universalism, joy, peace, lowliness, the poor of Yahweh seen in the shepherds, glory, today, and, of course, the person of Mary, the mother of Jesus.

Mary and Joseph go up to Bethlehem from Nazareth to be enrolled. This is Luke's way of associating the birth of Jesus with a Davidic town. Matthew had the family possessing a home in Bethlehem. This town was the one in which David began his reign as king for seven years, while spending thirty-three as king in Jerusalem. Luke does not link Mary to the family of David; it is only through Joseph that Jesus is a Davidid. The Marian emphasis is especially seen in the last two lines of the birth account where Mary in giving birth to Jesus wraps him in swaddling clothes and lays him in a manger. Swaddling was done to help the child's correct growth and to keep him warm. The simplicity and realism of this event are in stark contrast to the docetic exaggerations of the Apocryphal Gospels.

Jesus is called "firstborn" (*prototokos*), not the only born son (*monogenes*). Does Luke, therefore, imply Mary had other children? The term "firstborn" is used even if there is only one child born to the mother. Luke is mentioning this in order to have Mary fulfill the laws of purification which he will narrate in the Presentation scene (Lk 2: 22-38).

The Shepherds and the Angels: Luke 2:8-20

> [8]In that region there were shepherds living in the fields,
>   keeping watch over their flock by night.
> [9]Then an angel of the Lord stood before them, and the glory
>   of the Lord shone around them, and they were
>   terrified.
> [10]But the angel said to them, "Do not be afraid; for see — I
>   am bringing you good news of great joy for all the
>   people:

¹¹to you is born this day in the city of David a Savior, who is
the Messiah, the Lord.
¹²This will be a sign for you: you will find a child wrapped in
bands of cloth and lying in a manger."
¹³And suddenly there was with the angel a multitude of the
heavenly host, praising God and saying,
¹⁴"Glory to God in the highest heaven, and on earth peace
among those whom he favors!"
¹⁵When the angels had left them and gone into heaven, the
shepherds said to one another, "Let us now go to
Bethlehem and see this thing that has taken place,
which the Lord has made known to us."
¹⁶So they went with haste and found Mary and Joseph, and
the child lying in the manger.
¹⁷When they saw this, they made known what had been told
them about this child;
¹⁸and all who heard it were amazed at what the shepherds
told them.
¹⁹But Mary treasured all these words and pondered them in
her heart.
²⁰The shepherds returned, glorifying and praising God for all
they had heard and seen, as it had been told them.

Our Marian references in this scene come near the end, but
like all of Luke's passages, several of the principal themes are
reiterated in a new context. His universalism is seen in the presence
of the lowly shepherds who are made aware of the great event by an
angel and then by a vision of the whole angelic host praising and
glorifying God. Both the earth and heaven are involved in this
universalism. Luke also mentions that this is good news (salvation)
for all the people. The structure of the pericope is typically Lucan
in this section of his Gospel, for again we have an Annunciation
schema followed by a hymn. It parallels what has happened to Mary
in chapter one. Like Mary the shepherds go with haste to find out
about this word or event. The other themes common to this Gospel
found here are the joy, the glory given to God, God's favor on
people, the lowly, Mary and Joseph, today, and the prayerful

dimension of praise and reflection. Mary continues to be central to these scenes. Luke introduces the shepherds to Mary while the angels continue to praise Jesus as Savior, Messiah, and Lord. Mary has already heard these titles from Gabriel but now even the lowly shepherds are aware of them.

It is Mary who is emphasized as the scene closes. She ponders over (*symballousa*) these (*a remata* = events, things — words from the Hebrew equivalent *dabar*) things that the shepherds announce to her and Joseph and the people. There is a continued and developing trust and hope expressed in this pericope both on the part of the shepherds and on the part of Mary who sees and listens to their message. Luke will close his earliest reflections on Jesus with Mary's pondering over the scene in the temple (Lk 2:51).[8] These two phrases describing Mary pondering over these sacred events which surround Jesus, her son, as an infant and as a young man, are important signposts. She ponders over all these things in her heart. Both Fitzmyer and van Unnik see a conative force in the expression *symballousa* and see Mary as "trying to hit upon the right meaning." However, Fitzmyer and Brown caution that the reader should not posit Mary as a direct source for Luke's Gospel for the third generation of Christians These personal insights come from the third stage of Gospel development, namely, from the evangelist himself and his theological interests as well as kerygmatic purposes.

In the chapter on Luke's Gospel in *Mary in the New Testament* we find this important interpretation: "In 2:19 'all these things' involve what the shepherds have told about the angelic revelation; but in 2:51 nothing patently miraculous is involved — there 'all these things' refer to the finding of Jesus and his rebuff to his parents, when he placed primacy on his duty toward his Father. What the two scenes have in common is a revelation, explicit or implicit, about the future of the child. The emphasis is not on facts, but on significance" (*MNT*, p. 148). We therefore continue to see Mary growing in her life of discipleship as she progresses with the infant to whom she has given birth. The motherhood of Mary is closely related to her call as a believing disciple; both aspects involved not only the joy and grace of God, but also the necessity of suffering, reflecting, and living out this call to motherhood and discipleship.

The Naming of Jesus and the Presentation in the Temple: Luke 2:21-40

21After eight days had passed, it was time to circumcise the child; and he was called Jesus, the name given by the angel before he was conceived in the womb.

22When the time came for their purification according to the law of Moses, they brought him up to Jerusalem to present him to the Lord

23(as it is written in the law of the Lord, "Every firstborn male shall be designated as holy to the Lord"),

24and they offered a sacrifice according to what is stated in the law of the Lord, "a pair of turtledoves or two young pigeons."

25Now there was a man in Jerusalem whose name was Simeon; this man was righteous and devout, looking forward to the consolation of Israel, and the Holy Spirit rested on him.

26It had been revealed to him by the Holy Spirit that he would not see death before he had seen the Lord's Messiah.

27Guided by the Spirit, Simeon came into the temple; and when the parents brought in the child Jesus, to do for him what was customary under the law,

28Simeon took him in his arms and praised God, saying,

29"Master, now you are dismissing your servant in peace, according to your word;

30for my eyes have seen your salvation,

31which you have prepared in the presence of all peoples,

32a light for revelation to the Gentiles and for glory to your people Israel."

33And the child's father and mother were amazed at what was being said about him.

34Then Simeon blessed them and said to his mother Mary,

"This child is destined for the falling and the rising of
many in Israe , and to be a sign that will be opposed
[35]so that the inner thoughts of many will be revealed — and
a sword will pierce your own soul too."
[36]There was also a prophetess, Anna, the daughter of
Phanuel, of the tribe of Asher. She was of great age,
having lived with her husband seven years after her
marriage,
[37]then as a widow to the age of eighty-four. She never left
the temple but worshipped there with fasting and
prayer night and day.
[38]At that moment she came, and began to praise God and to
speak about the child to all who were looking for the
redemption of Jerusalem.
[39]When they had finished everything required by the law of
the Lord, they returned to Galilee, to their own town
of Nazareth.
[40]The child grew and became strong, filled with wisdom; and
the favor of God was upon him.

This is Luke's account of a fourth episode in which Mary is
center-stage. The recalling of the joyful mysteries of the rosary will
help to construct the five scenes in which Mary is present: the
Annunciation, the Visitation, the Nativity, the Presentation, and
the Finding of Jesus in the Temple. Both E. LaVerdiere and J.
Fitzmyer offer cogent reasons for including the circumcision and
the naming of the child as part of this fourth episode. The naming
is more important for Luke; the circumcision continues the parallel
to the Baptist narrative in chapter one and helps us to see more
clearly the literary diptych that Luke presents to us. Both Testaments show us the importance of a name which not only identifies
a person but especially shows the character and mission as well for
that person. Luke continues to write an imitative historiography
which is based on the Samuel narrative (1 S 1:22-24) for this
section.[9]

Both Fitzmyer and LaVerdiere also have a similar outline for
this section: v. 21 serves as an initiating prelude, vv. 22-24 depict a

second prelude to the purification and presentation. Then follows the second main part in the double manifestation of Jesus to Simeon and Anna (vv. 25-35; 36-38); vv. 39-40 form a conclusion through the return to Nazareth. This also forms a type of an inclusion in the journey to and from Jerusalem.

This pericope also offers a plethora of Lucan themes and symbols that keep the reader aware of Luke's theology. Together with the initial chapter of Luke we have a type of showcase for Luke-Acts in these themes and symbols. What are they? Promise-fulfill-ment, universalism, the poor of God, Jerusalem, Temple, Spirit, Israel, the Gentiles, Jesus as Messiah and Lord, another canticle, a blessing, prayer, deliverance, God's favor, peace, glory, and Mary.

In verses 21-24, Luke shows the parents of Jesus fulfilling all the prescriptions of the Mosaic Law just as the parents of the Baptist had done. Both sets of parents are seen as righteous people graced by God. The notion of the Law being fulfilled occurs five times within this section. It sets the atmosphere within Judaism which is now being fulfilled in these saintly persons and in the Messiah Jesus. It has been pointed out by most exegetes that Luke is not accurate in how he describes the law of purification. That is not his interest in his description of "their" purification. Rather, the theological point he is making is that the Spirit leads all who are mentioned by name in these first chapters to fulfill God's law and God's revelation by their fidelity both to the letter and spirit. This obedience to God's word will continue to be the basic attitude of Mary who gave her *fiat* to the angel and continues to do so as a faithful disciple in this Gospel.

From a historical-critical point of view, Luke is not recalling what Mary said to him, but is directing the narrative according to his own theological intentions. He does not focus on later Church concerns such as the virginity of Mary. In fact, the direct use of the language from the Hebrew Scriptures is quite descriptive and beckons all Christian reflection on the virginity of Mary to remain close to the Gospel texts and away from any form of docetism or the fantasizing so prevalent in the Apocryphal Gospels. From Luke's presentation in this scene we are impressed with the natural manner of Jesus' birth of his human mother. We are not thereby denying her virginity, but we are also not focusing on biological descriptions or docetic falsehoods about the birth. Fitzmyer, who edited the material on this section in the book *Mary in the New Testament* puts it clearly in this way, "Although this phrase ("a male who opens the womb," Lk 2:22) has created a problem in the discussion of the later Christian idea that Mary gave *birth* to Jesus miraculously (*virginitas in partu*), without rupture of the hymen, Luke may be employing standard O.T. language (see Exod 13:2, 12, 15 in the LXX) and telling us nothing specific about the manner of Jesus' birth" (*MNT*, p. 153). Plummer states: 'The *dianoigon metran* (the opening of the womb) seems to be fatal to patristic speculations respecting Mary's having given birth to the Christ *clauso utero*, and therefore painlessly" (*International Critical Commentary: Luke*, A. Plummer, p. 65).

The Purification refers to the mother; the Presentation to the child Jesus. In the context, the Presentation is what is important, that is, they brought him to present him to the Lord. All of the important manuscripts read in the plural "for their purification." It is more accurate to understand the Jewish law as speaking only of the mother's purification. The father was not included, nor the child. Luke, however, is focusing more on the Presentation than on Purification.

Simeon appears on the scene in verse 25. His name is a common one and through popular etymology means "Yahweh has heard." The first Simeon mentioned in the Bible was one of the sons of Jacob and Leah; hence, one of the twelve tribes of Israel. We need not suppose that the Simeon mentioned in Luke is advanced in age though popular opinion presumes he is and this is true of most artists' conceptions of Simeon as well. He together with Anna, the prophetess, are holy persons dedicated to God through prayer and frequentation of the temple. It is not through a vision or dream but through God's revelation in this event that Simeon realizes the promises made to him are fulfilled in the Messiah Jesus. He is so overwhelmed that he takes the child in his arms and praises God in his canticle while losing sight of all else that surrounds him.

It is interesting to note that the Church has continued to use all of Luke's canticles in the Liturgy of the Hours and the Eucharistic liturgy, keeping the order of the evangelist: Morning Praise, the Benedictus; Eucharist, the Gloria; Evening Prayer, the Magnificat; Night Prayer, the Nunc Dimittis. The canticle contains many of the Lucan themes: peace, salvation, universality, and promise and fulfillment. This is also the high point of the scene; Luke's message is conveyed through this hymn. This canticle also contains the first of two blessings in this section and is addressed to God.

The second blessing is bestowed by Simeon specifically on Mary the mother of Jesus. We have seen that Gabriel and then Elizabeth have already proclaimed her blessed; now the devout Simeon brings a "mixed blessing" upon Mary because of the mission and destiny of her child. The expression used for a sword symbolizes more anguish than the pain of contradictory thoughts or decisions, although scholars, exegetes, and the Fathers of the Church lean toward the latter. The word *rhomphaia* means a long pike, a large sword rather than the ordinary weapon, hence, anguish is appropriate. Both Brown and Fitzmyer have recourse to Ezekiel 14:17 to interpret our passage. The oracle definitely is oriented toward the future of the child and how the mother will be involved in this painful falling and rising of many because of the child.

This javelin of anguish then passes through Mary's innermost being or her "soul." Is it the pain that she will endure because of her Son's own suffering, death, and almost total rejection? Or is it a sign of her own growth through difficult decisions about her own understanding of who Jesus is? There is no evidence of Mary at the foot of the Cross in Luke, yet we know that she did follow Jesus, for her last appearance is in the upper room shortly after the death of her Son. She also had the custom of going up to Jerusalem when Jesus was younger as we know from the Infancy Narrative. Modern exegetes and theologians side more with the theme of Mary's growth in faith as a disciple; the earlier tradition is to associate her with Jesus' sufferings as the Mater Dolorosa. As is often the case, it is best to respect both interpretations in reflecting on this passage. It is a question of a "both . . . and" rather than an "either . . . or."

The prophetess Anna enters the scene, thus balancing the appearance of Simeon. She can be conjectured to be either 104 years old or 84 depending upon how one reads the texts. It seems that both moderns and ancients prefer the 84 years. One ancient writer, Hesychius of Jerusalem, uses Psalm 84 in his reflection on this part of Luke's Gospel. Luke continues to use the background of 1 Samuel 1 and 2 for this part of his Infancy Narrative. Hanna, the mother of Samuel, is also found in the temple, searching for fulfillment of God's promises to her as a woman. Anna, inspired by the Spirit, comes to meet the parents of Jesus while she too praises God and speaks of the child who is God's way of redemption for her people.

Anna was one among many women prophetesses: Sarah; Miriam (Ex 15:20); Deborah (Jg 4:4); Hannah, mother of Samuel (1 S 2:1); Abigail, wife of David (1 S 25:32); Huldah (2 K 22:14); and Esther. In the tradition and devotion of the Church to Mary, we will see that many of these women were seen as symbols for the person of Mary, the mother of Jesus. All these women are considered to be saintly, prophetic, and accomplishers of God's will. Anna is one of the devout widows who pointed out the Messiah by her coming to the temple. We might also take note that from the apocryphal Gospel of James we will learn that Mary's own mother is called Anna.

Luke brings the Infancy Narrative to a close with verses 39-40 which serve both as a summary statement and an inclusion. Verse 40 parallels what was said about the Baptist except that Jesus is not said to grow in the Spirit. Probably, Luke already understands Jesus as possessing the fullness of the Spirit in light of the Annunciation to Mary (Lk 1:35).

The Boy Jesus in the Temple: Luke 2:41-52

[41]Now every year his parents went to Jerusalem for the festival of the Passover.
[42]And when he was twelve years old, they went up as usual for the festival.
[43]When the festival was ended and they started to return, the boy Jesus stayed behind in Jerusalem, but his parents did not know it.
[44]Assuming that he was in the group of travelers, they went a day's journey. Then they started to look for him among their relatives and friends.
[45]When they did not find him, they returned to Jerusalem to search for him.
[46]After three days they found him in the temple, sitting among the teachers, listening to them and asking them questions.
[47]And all who heard him were amazed at his understanding and his answers.
[48]When his parents saw him they were astonished; and his mother said to him, "Child, why have you treated us like this? Look, your father and I have been searching for you in great anxiety."
[49]He said to them, "Why were you searching for me? Did you not know that I must be in my Father's house?"
[50]But they did not understand what he said to them.
[51]Then he went down with them and came to Nazareth, and was obedient to them. His mother treasured all these things in her heart.
[52]And Jesus increased in wisdom and in years, and in divine and human favor.

This passage is definitely independent of the rest of the Infancy Narrative. It serves as a transition from the infancy of Jesus to a reflection on his hidden years at Nazareth before his baptism as a mature adult: "Jesus was about thirty years of age when he began his work" (Lk 3:23). Unlike the Apocryphal Gospels which describe

Jesus at the age of five, eight, and twelve, Luke's account is more realistic and theological than the exaggerated miraculous and vulgar descriptions of those works that describe the adolescent Jesus (e.g., the Infancy Gospel of Thomas).

Luke depends on a tradition for this story, but recasts it in his own style and theology. It is not a legend. Rather Luke continues his development of Jesus through a type of literary and imitative historiography based on the story of the young Samuel (1 S 1:3, 21; 2:19; 3:3). The Christological focus of Luke is what is most important in this narrative. This is evident in the first words spoken by Jesus in this Gospel which are given in the form of two questions: "Why are you searching for me? Did you not know that I must be in my Father's house?" (Lk 2:49). Jesus' first words in the Fourth Gospel are a question, "What are you looking for?" (Jn 1:38) and an invitation, "Come and see" (Jn 1:39). Those closest to Jesus, his parents (Mary and Joseph), are also central to this narrative for they stimulate the atmosphere with their search, their misunderstanding, their anguish, and their questions. The story line therefore is built around the words of Jesus which are indicative of his relationship on a most intimate level with God, whom he refers to as "my Father." Fitzmyer calls this a "pronouncement story" while Brown says it is a "biographical apothegm," but both emphasize it as the illustration of a Christological saying shaped out of a life setting.

There are similarities in this narrative story to what is found in the Cana account in John 2:1-11, which also takes place before the active ministry of Jesus. Mary, too, is involved in stimulating a revelation on the part of Jesus; here it is more through a sign than through a statement.

In line with the instruction on the *Historical Truth of the Gospels*, we are dealing with the third stage of Gospel material, that is, Luke's own final redaction of the text in the third generation after the death of Jesus. We are not speaking of memoirs of Mary given personally to Luke. We are dealing with how the evangelist makes use of the traditional material he has received, that is, with the Gospel context for the saying or event that is related (see Instruction, part V). This enables us to give a better foundation for our Christology and Mariology when we proceed from the text rather than from the insights of Church dogma or from systematic theology. Luke's Christology is one which uses the titles that are appropriate to the Resurrected Christ but are placed into the baptism of Jesus, then to his adolescence, and finally into the birth narrative and conception of Jesus. This is the point that Fitzmyer is making as he concludes his remarks on the Infancy Narrative: "Furthermore, in certain circles of systematic theology today, people are seeking to substitute for a 'christology from above' a so-called 'christology from below.' Say what one will about the legitimacy of this distinction and of the later understanding of Jesus, one has to realize that the Lucan infancy narrative, like that of Matthew, knows only a 'christology from above.' That is the whole point of the 'revelation' that is made to Mary, to the shepherds, and to Jesus' parents (indirectly) by the child in the Temple himself" (*Luke: Anchor Bible*, Vol. 28, p. 447).

One of the concerns for Mariologists is the fact that Mary does not seem to understand who Jesus is through the questions and the misunderstanding and anguish she experiences when she discovers Jesus in the temple. "Child, why have you treated us like this? Look, your father and I have been searching for you in great anxiety" (Lk 2:48). At the Annunciation she seems to have been flooded with all sorts of information and insights into the grandeur of her son. Here, in the Temple scene, this is not the case. It shows us another aspect of how Mary, too, grows gradually in faith as a believer in the person of Jesus. Rather than give her a preternatural type of knowledge, Luke renders her more human, more real through the experience of a mother who has lost her child and does not comprehend his behavior when he has been found. This is important for our own way of growing in faith and understanding of who Jesus is. Mary becomes a model for us that is not on a superior plane but one who experiences our own struggles in coming to understand who Jesus is in our lives and in his relationship to God. The story is important, as it is the only one that deals with the teenage period of Jesus, thus offering both parents and teenagers an important biblical revelation about this troublesome period of events and growth patterns.

Jesus is no longer being spoken about in God's revelation. It is he himself who tells us about who he is in relation to God. The sacredness of the temple precinct offers the location for this first direct revelation of Jesus who is concerned about his listening to God his Father and accomplishing the mission he is being prepared for. The transition to his active ministry is thus highlighted by this pronouncement. It happens in the temple, just as the opening of this Gospel begins with the temple and just as the Gospel concludes with it in Luke 24:53 and then continues in the story of the Church in Acts. Mary, too, is experiencing what Simeon had foretold, "and a sword will pierce your own soul too" (Lk 2:35). She will continue to experience this as she hears about or follows her son on the great journey to Jerusalem again, only this time in his Exodus to the Father. She will show that she matures as a believer as we find her mentioned for the last time in Luke's writings (in Acts 1:14) in the room upstairs as she awaits again the coming of the Spirit. All of this is in keeping with the Divine necessity that Luke is so fond of developing. He indicates this by his use of *dei* (must, need to be, etc.) in v. 49: "I must be in my Father's house." Fitzmyer says, "It expresses not only a necessity in general, but the peculiar Lucan connotation of what had to be as part of the Father's salvific plan" (*Luke*, p. 443, and p. 180).

Luke brings in a Marian refrain in verse 51 which attests to her growth in understanding Jesus as more than her natural son and to her ability to sound the depths of meaning in the events and the words that involve her son Jesus. He then concludes with another Jesus refrain which parallels that of the Baptist, namely, that he increased in wisdom and in years and in divine and human favor.

Luke, more than any other evangelist, has clearly marked out the growth of Jesus from the moment of conception as a Holy One of God (Lk 1:31, 35) (prenatal), to a baby (2:16 = *brephos*) lying in the manger, to an infant (2:40 = *paidion*) being presented in the temple, to the boy being found in the temple (2:43 = *pais*), and finally to his being about thirty years old and identified as the "son of Joseph" (Lk 3:23). Luke has also depicted Mary as the believer who continues her journey of faith from the Annunciation to the descent of the Spirit in the upper room.

The Rejection at Nazareth: Luke 4:16-30
(Parallels in Mt 13:54-58; Mk 6:1-6)

16When he came to Nazareth, where he had been brought up, he went to the synagogue on the Sabbath day, as was his custom. He stood up to read,

17and the scroll of the prophet Isaiah was given to him. He unrolled the scroll and found the place where it was written:

18"The Spirit of the Lord is upon me, because he has anointed me to bring good news to the poor. He has sent me to proclaim release to the captives and recovery of sight to the blind, to let the oppressed go free,

19to proclaim the year of the Lord's favor."

20And he rolled up the scroll, gave it back to the attendant, and sat down. The eyes of all in the synagogue were fixed on him.

21Then he began to say to them, "Today this Scripture has been fulfilled in your hearing."

22All spoke well of him and were amazed at the gracious words that came from his mouth. They said, "Is not this Joseph's son?"

23He said to them, "Doubtless you will quote to me this proverb, `Doctor, cure yourself!' And you will say, `Do here in your hometown the things that we have heard you did at Capernaum.'"

24And he said, "Truly I tell you, no prophet is accepted in the prophet's hometown.

25But the truth is, there were many widows in Israel in the time of Elijah, when the heaven was shut up three years and six months, and there was a severe famine over all the land;

²⁶yet Elijah was sent to none of them except to a widow at Zarephath in Sidon.
²⁷There were also many lepers in Israel in the time of the prophet Elisha, and none of them was cleansed except Naaman the Syrian."
²⁸When they heard this, all in the synagogue were filled with rage.
²⁹They got up, drove him out of the town, and led him to the brow of the hill on which their town was built, so that they might hurl him off the cliff.
³⁰But he passed through the midst of them and went on his way.

In verse 22 of this passage, Jesus' family is referred to in the words, "Is not this Joseph's son?" The pericope also shows the first opposition to Jesus who acts as a prophet in his own hometown. The similarities to the scenes from Matthew 13:54-58 and Mark 6:1-6 are apparent especially in the description of the people and their opinion of Jesus (the *Sitz im Leben* or life situation); yet, all three evangelists have placed this incident differently in their Gospels and have a different theological perspective on Jesus (see H. Anderson, *Interpretation* 18 [1964], 259-275; D. Hill, *Novum Testamentum* 13 [1971], 161-180). Luke may have worked with an independent tradition or source about this occasion for he leaves out the reference to Mary, the brothers and the sisters of Jesus, and to the carpenter whether applied to Jesus or Joseph. There is also a remarkable parallel in John 6:42 where the crowd also questions Jesus' origins but are convinced he is only the son of Joseph. Both John and Luke may have the same theological perspective in their irony of showing that Jesus is really the Son of God while the people think of him as the son of Joseph.

In the book *Mary in the New Testament* we have an excellent summary about this passage from Luke: "In general, Luke is kinder to those who surround Jesus than is either Mark or Matthew; but his sensitivity toward Jesus' relatives and household may be more than an example of general benevolence. The mother who has been praised in 1:38, 42, 45 and 2:19, 51 as one who heard the word of God and did it and as one who kept and retained the mysterious sayings about Jesus that she heard could scarcely fit the category of those who did not accept Jesus. Neither could the brothers of Jesus whom, along with the mother, Luke will present as following Jesus (Ac 1:14). Thus, once again, the scene adds no Marian import to the picture of Jesus' ministry; but neither does it detract from Luke's positive picture of Jesus' mother" (*MNT*, pp. 166-167).

Jesus' True Relatives: Luke 8:19-21
(Parallels in Mt 12:46-50; Mk 3:31-35)

> [19]Then his mother and his brothers came to him, but they
>   could not reach him because of the crowd.
> [20]And he was told, "Your mother and your brothers are
>   standing outside, wanting to see you."
> [21]But he said to them, "My mother and my brothers are those
>   who hear the word of God and do it."

Contemporaneous exegetes have placed this saying or *macarism* of Jesus within the context of the parable of the sower and the lamp. Particularly appropriate is the conclusion of the parable of the sower: "But as for that in the good soil, these are the ones who, when they hear the word, hold it fast in an honest and good heart, and bear fruit with patient endurance" (Lk 8:15). Luke thus gives a unique context to the statement of Jesus, "My mother and my brothers are those who hear the word of God and do it" (Lk 8:21). This contextual reading then interprets Mary and Jesus' brothers as fulfilling in their lives what the parables point out and call forth from the believer. Thus Mary and the brothers are believing disciples in Luke. The two parables tend to veil and at the same time illustrate a reality or truth about those who believe and put into practice what they believe. Mary and the brothers are those who listen to and do the will of God. Thus they are a part of Jesus' eschatological or Kingdom family. They are like the good soil and good seed which both hold and produce. Mary and the brothers hold on to Jesus' words and accomplish them with a noble and generous heart. This is true discipleship in Luke.

True Blessedness: Luke 11:27-28

[27]While he was saying this, a woman in the crowd raised her voice and said to him, "Blessed is the womb that bore you and the breasts that nursed you!"
[28]But he said, "Blessed rather are those who hear the word of God and obey it!"

Luke is the evangelist of beatitudes and in this final Gospel passage about Mary there is another beatitude conferred upon her that confirms those given in the Infancy Narrative at the Annunciation and Visitation. This passage is the biblical basis for giving Mary the appellation Blessed Mother (see my remarks above on Lk 1:42-45). Fitzmyer summarizes this beatitudinal thrust of Luke: "In Luke 1:45, Elizabeth made it clear that Mary was 'blessed' or an object of praise, not just because she was to be Jesus' mother, but because she had believed what had been told to her was to be fulfilled by the Lord. Similarly, here, the second beatitude is phrased generically, praising 'those who hear and observe,' and states a reason for their happiness. The second does not negate the first, but formulates rather what Jesus considers of prime importance and merely corrects the inadequacy of the first" (*Luke: Anchor Bible*, p. 927). Besides the sorrow that Mary will experience, we see that Luke's image of her is one of an optimistic and happy servant of God's word and the mother of Jesus who is truly blessed naturally and eschatologically.

This proclamation story is independent of the above scene and is taken from "Q" material or a sayings source that Luke used. Jesus is raising the level of understanding who really are blessed compared to the laudatory cry of the woman about Jesus' naturally blessed mother. Luke keeps the two beatitudes in line with what Mary said in her Magnificat and within the present context of chapter 11, namely, that true beatitude consists not in exorcisms or words but in fruitfulness and obedience to the word of God.

A Lucan Summary and his Last Mention of Mary: Acts 1:12-14

> [12]Then they returned to Jerusalem from the mount called Olivet, which is near Jerusalem, a Sabbath day's journey away.
> [13]When they had entered the city, they went to the room upstairs where they were staying, Peter, and John, and James, and Andrew, Philip and Thomas, Bartholomew and Matthew, James son of Alphaeus, and Simon the Zealot, and Judas son of James.
> [14]All these were constantly devoting themselves to prayer, together with certain women, including Mary the mother of Jesus, as well as his brothers.

This is the final mention of Mary in Luke's work entitled the Acts of the Apostles. The verses above are considered to be one of the summaries that Luke gives to the reader at definite places within the Acts. The fact that Luke-Acts is the work of one writer gives us a fabric of texts which can facilitate our comparison of what we know about Mary from the first volume (Luke) and the final mention of her in the second volume (Acts). The image of Mary and the image of the Church in the Acts cannot be separated from what we know about her and the disciples in the Gospel.

What is important for our consideration of Mary within this passage is the fact that Luke considers what is to happen in the upper room, namely, the coming of the Holy Spirit upon the believers, as a parallel to his Infancy Narrative. The birth of the Church is basically the presentation of the power of the Spirit of Jesus upon the apostles, Mary, and the brothers and sisters of Jesus. The life of Jesus was similarly announced by the power of the Spirit upon the Virgin Mary at the Annunciation (Lk 1:26-38). Both births occur at the beginning of each of Luke's major writings and are both under the shadow and power of the Holy Spirit. The literary genres used are different for the birth of Jesus and the birth of the Church, but the content and message are the same. Mary was told, "The Holy Spirit will come upon you and the power of the Most High will overshadow you; hence, the holy offspring to be born will be called Son of God" (Lk 1:35). The faithful followers of Jesus are told not to leave Jerusalem for "within a few days you will be baptized with the Holy Spirit" (Ac 1:5). They, in turn, will continue the mission of Jesus: "You will receive power when the Holy Spirit comes down on you; then you are to be my witnesses in Jerusalem, throughout Judea and Samaria, yes, even to the ends of the earth" (Ac 1:8).

There is evidence that the group gathered in the upper room are the disciples who are mentioned in Acts 1:2. Eleven are named and are also called apostles elsewhere (Lk 6:13). Mary, the mother of Jesus, is named, while the women and the "brethren" are merely mentioned. All of them are together united in prayer. This element of praying together in the synagogue, in the upper room, and elsewhere, is characteristic of the emerging Church in the Acts of the Apostles. We have seen how Mary is a model of faith and prayer in the Gospel (cf. her dialogue with the angel, 1:26-38; her song of praise, 1:46-55; and her reflective mind and heart, 2:19 and 2:51). Her presence in the upper room is more than symbolic. Among all the names mentioned in Acts 1:13, she is the person who actually has given witness to a prayer life modeled on the Psalms and to a personal reflective prayer. Though we know the disciples frequented the temple at the hours of prayer, she alone gives us the content of her prayer through her personal pondering over the events and words (*rhemata*) in the early life of her son. She is now a model for the apostles and disciples and friends of Jesus gathered in the upper room. If later the twelve decide to continue devoting themselves to prayer and to the ministry of the word, it is evident their gathering in the upper room was a significant experience at the inception of the Church. Mary shared in that prayer with them and the gathered ones. Before the Spirit descended upon them, prayer was what united them; after the coming of the Spirit, prayer continued among the followers of Jesus.

Mary is a model for the Church at prayer. It is clear from the text of Acts 1:14 that she was considered a full member of the group. People of "one mind" cannot possibly consider others as second class citizens. Mary is fully the Church inasmuch as the Church is at prayer. We have no further mention of her after this and there is no trace of her being sent out on a mission on this occasion. But prayer, too, is mission and it is here that Mary is a model "par excellence."

Frequently, Luke as an evangelist shares the same themes as the Fourth Gospel. With Mary's presence in the upper room, we have the only parallel of her being present after the death of Jesus in John 19:25-28a. The latter scene is bound into the ecclesiology of the Fourth Gospel and could give evidence that John, too, was aware of a tradition of the presence of Mary not at Calvary but at Pentecost when the Christian Church is born. The sign symbolism in chapter 19:25-28 of John is suggestive of the birth of the Church, while for Luke the gathering of the people of God waiting for the descent of the Spirit is evocative of the ecclesiology which will be so characteristic for the rest of the Acts.

The text in giving us the name of Mary places her in a special position to be representative of the Church at prayer (*ecclesia orans*). Though later in the Acts an upper room of another woman named Mary, the mother of John Mark, is mentioned, this is not in connection with what is happening in so dramatic a way in Acts 1 and 2. The woman who emerges as the best image of the Church in Luke is Mary the mother of Jesus. Luke-Acts as a two-volume work has a definite pattern of paralleling events from the first book with those of the second. Just as Mary was physically the mother of Jesus, so, too, she is actively there as the Church is being born on Pentecost. Through her prayer — a prayer of waiting and expectation of the fulfillment of the promises of the Risen Lord — Mary becomes again a dynamic instrument, or better, a consenting human person who disposes herself once again to receive the gift of the

Spirit just as she did at the Annunciation. The overshadowing of the Spirit brought about the birth of Jesus her son. Now the descent of the Holy Spirit impregnates all present in the upper room to preach and witness to their new birth as the community of Jesus or the "Church." Luke's universalism and concern for salvation history did not allow him to avoid mentioning Mary. She consistently has been a woman of faith and prayer from the Annunciation at Galilee, to the temple rites in Jerusalem, to the time of the Passover, and now finally in the upper room awaiting the descent of the Holy Spirit as Jesus had promised. Both in Luke and John we see that Mary is an important figure in the communities of these evangelists.

In Rudolf Bultmann's classic commentary on John, the text of Acts 1:14 is cited in connection with the final appearance of Jesus' mother in the Fourth Gospel. This bears out the scholar's contention that Mary was an important person in the Lucan and Johannine circles. Here, both evangelists converge to correct the impression taken from Mark and Matthew that she did not belong to the group of followers of Jesus. John solves the problem for Mary's faith in her son, but not for the brothers of Jesus (Jn 7:5). Luke, the universalist, has both the mother and the brothers together at Pentecost. Bultmann is convinced: "According to Acts 1:14, certainly, she belongs to the first community, along with the brothers of Jesus, although (in Luke) no mention is made of her relationship to the 'Beloved Disciple'" (*The Gospel of John: A Commentary*, p. 672).

In John's Gospel the interest is centered on only one woman, the mother of Jesus. Likewise, in Acts 1:14, Mary the mother of Jesus is the only woman named; thus, she is central to the purpose of this short summary text of Luke.

In my opinion, Luke gives an ecclesiological interpretation to Mary's presence with the eleven and the other hundred or so gathered in the upper room. She is named the model believer among women by Elizabeth (cf. Lk 1:45). She is that same believing and courageous woman who ushers in the age of the Church at Pentecost, just as she brought Jesus into our world's history as God's salvific agent. In John's Gospel, she alone is commissioned for such an ecclesiological role as woman; in Acts it is Mary the mother of Jesus who has a unique role in the founding of the first community of Christian Jews. Luke does not mention her name again, but her role, which was so clearly described in the Infancy Narrative, continues in the community that is being born. Bultmann interprets the scene at Calvary as symbolic for Church unity "that all may be one" (cf. Jn 17:21). Can we not see in the persevering prayer of the eleven with Mary, the women, and the brothers of Jesus the unified community that will also continue to persevere in oneness (*koinonia*)?

It is my conviction that Luke has used this summary and others in the Acts to show the development of the Church. These are, for the most part, accounts of his own ecclesiological concern and purpose in the Acts. His ecclesiology is represented principally in those areas which come directly from his summary statements about the emerging movement which will eventually be the universal Church.

It is significant, then, that Mary is mentioned in the very first of these summaries and thereby is linked to the Church or the first Christian community. She, as the only woman so named and as the mother of Jesus, is linked to the beginnings of Luke's story (Lk 1 and 2) and, as a memorable person, forms a continuity with Israel and the Jewish beginnings of the Church. She is a special presence in the nascent Church for she is "with" the apostles, and is "with" the women and the brothers of Jesus. The unity of this primitive community is achieved through dedication to prayer. Thus Mary is a model for the components of faith, prayer, and community. She nurtures as mother those gathered in the upper room, just as she nurtured the infant Jesus who would cause the fall and the rise of many in Israel (Lk 2:34). Luke portrays Mary as a woman who believes in the person of Jesus her son even beyond his death, while she unites in prayer with the other believers who await their empowerment from the promised Spirit of Jesus who will be born again in the Church, that is, in this community. She is the only woman who is called the mother of Jesus; could Luke be indicating that she is the only woman who could ever be called the mother of the Church, the first community of the believers of Jesus, the Christ?

From the context of Acts 1:14, Mary is an image of *ecclesia orans* (the praying community or Church). In the Gospel she was depicted as the youthful energetic virgin who was attentive to the Lord and who continued to praise God from the depths of her being. She continues to do this, pondering over the events of Jesus in her heart. Now in the upper room she is that fully matured woman who has experienced the sword of discrimination promised so long ago by Simeon (Lk 2:35); she continues to pray steadfastly with the women, the eleven, and the brothers of Jesus.

Allison A. Trites says Luke's "primary interest is to show that prayer is the instrument by which God has directed the course of holy history, both in the life of the Son of Man and in the development of the Christian Church" ("The Prayer Motif in Luke-Acts" in *Perspectives on Luke-Acts*, p. 169). Mary is central to the birth of the Son of Man; she is also central as woman to the birth of the Church. Her attitude of expectant prayer and constant prayer without losing heart (Lk 18:1) is present in both the Infancy Narrative and in the Church Narrative of Luke. For Luke and his intended readers, she is the person who, after the example of her son Jesus, models for believers the prayer of Israel and the prayer of the Church.

In the Gospel there are 19 mentions of prayer; in the Acts there are 25 significant passages about prayer. The birth of the Church is presented as a result of prayer. The disciples, Mary, the women and the brothers are told to return to Jerusalem to await the promise of the Spirit (Lk 24:49; Ac 1:4-5). In obeying Jesus, they gathered in an upper room (Ac 1:13) and were of one mind and one heart steadfast in prayer (Ac 1:14).

After ten days of prayer, came the feast of Pentecost and the Holy Spirit descended upon this community at prayer. Luke describes the results: "The new believers devoted themselves to the apostles' teaching and fellowship, to the breaking of the bread and the prayers" (Ac 2:42). Prayer was thus an integral part of the Christian movement from the start and its vitality was closely related in Luke's eyes to the growth of the Church (Ac 2:47). Mary was a central figure in that initial gathering that experienced the birth of the Church through the coming of the Spirit.

Conclusion to Luke's Imaging of Mary

It should be quite evident that the Gospel of Luke and the Acts give us the essential framework for the beginnings of an authentic study of Mary (Mariology). This Gospel is not a Mariolatry but a Christ-centered proclamation to Christian believers of all times. Mary, the mother of the Lord, is primarily a believer who has been with Jesus from his conception, to his birth, his infancy, childhood, and manhood. She continues as a believer after his death and is present when Jesus' promise of his Spirit is given at Pentecost. There is no one person who ever had such a close relationship with Jesus in all of these stages of his life and that of his Church. Luke has brought to us the mysteries of joy and those of sorrow through this believer. It is at Pentecost that she enters the mystery of the glory of the Risen Lord who is ever faithful to his promises. It is within this Lucan perspective that any study of Mary should begin, for he is the only evangelist who has through his own theological purpose developed this portrait of Mary as a woman of faith who speaks, prays, and listens in the name of her son Jesus.

Endnotes

1. H. J. Cadbury, *The Making of Luke-Acts* (Macmillan, New York, 1927).

L. Keck and J. L. Martyn, (eds.), *Studies in Luke-Acts* (Nashville/New York, Abingdon, 1966).

C. H. Talbert, *Literary Patterns, Theological Themes and the Genre of Luke-Acts* (Missoula: Scholars Press, 1974).

_____, (ed.), *Perspectives on Luke-Acts* (Danville, Virginia, 1978).

_____, (ed.), *Luke-Acts: New Perspectives from the Society of Biblical Literature Seminar* (New York: Crossroads, 1984).

R. Maddox, (ed. J. Rickes), *The Purpose of Luke-Acts* (Edinburgh: T & T Clark, 1982).

2. Bertrand Buby, S.M., "Mary, A Model of Ecclesia-Orans in Acts 1:14," *Marian Studies* 35 (1984), pp. 87-99.

3. R. E. Brown, *The Birth of the Messiah* (Garden City, New York: Doubleday, 1979).

4. J. A. Fitzmyer, *The Gospel According to Luke I-IX. The Anchor Bible* 28 (Garden City, New York: Doubleday, 1981).

_____, *The Gospel According to Luke X-XXIV. The Anchor Bible* 28A (Garden City, New York: Doubleday, 1985).

5. R. Laurentin, *Structure et Théologie de Luc I-II. Etudes Bibliques* (Paris: J. Gabalda, 1957).

6. I. de la Potterie, *Mary in the Mystery of the Covenant* (New York: Alba House. 1992), p. 11.

7. Mary Catherine Nolan, O.P., *Mary's Song: Canticle of a Liberated People*, unpublished thesis (International Marian Research Institute, University of Dayton, Ohio: 1992), pp. 12-42.

8. Bertrand Buby, S.M., "The Biblical Prayer of Mary," *Review for Religious*, vol. 39, 1980.

9. R. D. Nelson, "David: A Model for Mary in Luke?," *Biblical Theological Bulletin*, vol. 18, 1988, pp. 138-142.

Chapter Five

THE GOSPEL OF JOHN
AND THE MOTHER OF JESUS

The Texts

John 1:13:

"Who were born, not of blood or of the will of the flesh or of
the will of man, but of God."
In several ancient Latin manuscripts this reads: "who was born
not of blood or the will of the flesh or the will of man, but of God."

John 2:1-12: the Cana Account:

¹On the third day there was a wedding in Cana of Galilee,
and the mother of Jesus was there.
²Jesus and his disciples had also been invited to the wedding.
³When the wine gave out, the mother of Jesus said to him,
"They have no wine."
⁴And Jesus said to her "Woman, what concern is that to you
and to me? My hour has not yet come."
⁵His mother said to the servants, "Do whatever he tells you."
⁶Now standing there were six stone water jars for the Jewish
rites of purification, each holding twenty or thirty
gallons.
⁷Jesus said to them, "Fill the jars with water." And they filled
them to the brim.

⁸He said to them, "Now draw some out, and take it to the chief steward." So they took it.

⁹When the steward tasted the water that had become wine, and did not know where it came from (though the servants who had drawn the water knew), the steward called the bridegroom

¹⁰and said to him, "Everyone serves the good wine first, and then the inferior wine after the guests have become drunk. But you have kept the good wine until now."

¹¹Jesus did this, the first of his signs, in Cana of Galilee, and revealed his glory; and his disciples believed in him.

¹²After this he went down to Capernaum with his mother, his brothers, and his disciples; and they remained there a few days.

John 6:42: Jesus the Son of Joseph:

⁴²They were saying, "Is not this Jesus, the son of Joseph, whose father and mother we know? How can he now say, 'I have come down from heaven'?"

John 7:3-5: The Unbelief of Jesus' Brothers:

³So his brothers said to him, "Leave here and go to Judea so that your disciples also may see the works you are doing;

⁴for no one who wants to be widely known acts in secret. If you do these things, show yourself to the world."

⁵(For not even his brothers believed in him.)

John 7:41-43: Division among the People about the origins of the Messiah:

⁴¹Others said, "This is the Messiah." But some asked, "Surely the Messiah does not come from Galilee, does he?

⁴²Has not the scripture said that the Messiah is descended from David and comes from Bethlehem, the village where David lived?"

⁴³So there was a division in the crowd because of him.

John 8:41:

"You are indeed doing what your father does." They said to him, "We are not illegitimate children; we have one father, God himself."

John 19:25-28a: Mary and the Beloved Disciple at the
                 foot of the Cross:

[25]Meanwhile, standing near the cross of Jesus were his
    mother, and his mother's sister, Mary the wife of
    Clopas, and Mary Magdalene.
[26]When Jesus saw his mother and the disciple whom he loved
    standing beside her, he said to his mother, "Woman,
    here is your son."
[27]Then he said to the disciple, "Here is your mother." And
    from that hour the disciple took her into his own
    home.
[28]After this, when Jesus knew that all was now finished, he
    said (in order to fulfill the scripture), "I am thirsty."

Within the last three decades there has been a remarkable contribution of books and articles on the Fourth Gospel. In these writings there is first a serious historical-critical study of the Gospel, then a dedication to the evangelist's theology, and finally a discovery of the Johannine symbolism. More recently, a healthy tension between the historical and theological is being achieved through an understanding of the symbolism in this Gospel. All three perspectives are important in the interpretation of the Gospel of St. John. They provide a more integrated and holistic understanding of the various levels of Johannine thought. These methods are used for the entire study of John's Gospel, and can be used in our study of the person of Mary.

In all of the reflections in this book, the text of the Gospels is primary in importance and offers us the most information. In a special way, the text of John gives us evidence of some of the historical events in the life of Jesus and his followers and his family.

There are some scenes in John that are similar to those found in the Synoptics, but we have other texts which touch upon the events and sayings of Jesus that are independent of the Synoptics and which offer us a profound contemplation of Jesus and those who surround him. This is due to the fact that John is the last of the Gospels. There are also remembrances of traditions about Jesus and his followers and family which were not recorded elsewhere. The text of John, therefore, is of primary importance for it is the foundation for the Incarnation and for the highest Christology in the New Testament. The text presents us with a new theology of Jesus given in the tradition of John the evangelist. Finally, the tension between what is found in the text (what is given) and how it is read by the believers (the Church) presents a certain symbolism which enriches our insights and knowledge of Jesus, his family, and his followers. It is evident from the texts themselves that Mary is presented in a positive way and is among those who believe in the person of Jesus and witness to him.

The Johannine community is thus later than that of Luke and Matthew. This Gospel reflects a different attitude toward Jesus and the authority he left his followers than that of the other writings of the New Testament. In the Fourth Gospel we have more a community of friendship, a *koinonia*, than a structured assembly of believers. In the Gospel itself we move quickly from the crowds in the first part of John to the more intimate friends who gather around Jesus in the second part. Some of these persons may be symbolic, others historical. We pass from Nicodemus to the Samaritan woman, to Martha and Mary and Lazarus; then to the Beloved Disciple, Mary Magdalene and Mary, the Mother of Jesus.

The Gospel as we now have it may have gone through as many as five redactions, but the inner structure of the themes and symbolisms have remained constant and are the product of a mind that has remembered the historical traditions relating to Jesus Christ and then profoundly reflected upon their meaning for the Christian community.

There is no great dependency on the former Gospels except

in some of the common tradition-material. The fourth evangelist is a theologian in his own r ght. It is he who directs our thought to the reality of the Incarnation and to the divinity of Jesus, the Word of God. The pre-existence of the Word is immediately affirmed in the opening lines of this Gospel. The Gospel is easily divided into:

> the Prologue: 1:1-18
> the Book of Signs: 1:19-12:50
> the Book of Glory: 13:1-19:42
> the Resurrection Narratives: chapters 20-21

The evangelist is clear about his purpose in the two endings of this Gospel:

In John 20:30-31:

> [30]Now Jesus did many other signs in the presence of his
> disciples, which are not written in this book.
> [31]But these are written so that you may come to believe that
> Jesus is the Messiah, the Son of God, and that
> through believing you may have life in his name.

And in John 21:24-25:

> [24]This is the disciple who is testifying to these things and has
> written them, and we know his testimony is true.
> [25]But there are also many other things that Jesus did; if every
> one of them were written down, I suppose that the
> world itself could not contain the books that would be
> written.

Our task will be to s tuate the passages on Mary given above within the overall context and purpose of the Fourth Gospel. The two principal scenes fall in both the first part (the Book of Signs) and the second part (the Book of Glory) of the Gospel, that is, the Cana Narrative (2:1-12) and the Calvary Scene (19:25-27).

The Fourth Gospel focuses on faith in the Book of Signs, and love in the Book of Glory. These themes of the Gospel are expressed through the active dynam sm of the two verbs *pisteuein* (active and personal trust and belief in the person of Jesus) and *agapan* (the perfecting and completing love of Jesus for the Father and for his disciples).[1] Faith and love are at the center of the disciples' commitment to Jesus the Revealer. Faith in the Gospel of John is the response of an open and enlightened mind and heart that turns toward the person of Jesus, the Word. Love is the energy of one's whole heart and person turned toward the other and to God. The Gospel is one of absolute decision for the person of Jesus through this faith and love commitment. "The one who puts faith in him (God's Son) does not come under judgment; but the unbeliever has already been judged in that allegiance is not given to God's only Son" (Jn 3:18). The theme of believing is shown by the use of the verb *pisteuein* which occurs 98 times within this Gospel (it is used 241 times in the New Testament). The theme of love is expressed through the verb *agapan* which is found 36 times in John (141 times in the entire New Testament). What is remarkable is that the verb for believing is found 76 times in the Book of Signs (chapters 1-12); it is found 22 times in the Book of Glory (chapters 13-21). This shows that the signs of Jesus are meant to lead us to belief in his person. In the Book of Glory the verb *agapan* appears 31 times and only 7 times in the Book of Signs. Clearly, the commitment of love is the key emphasis in the latter part of the Gospel.

John's theme of faith which permeates all of the seven signs of this Gospel is meant for those who are approaching Jesus for the first time or for those who are growing through and beyond the signs. Faith is only the beginning; the fullness of Christian commitment to Jesus and the Father is through love or *agape*. Father George MacRae says of the conclusion of John's Gospel that "to elicit faith and thus make eternal life possible, there were many other signs (seven were given in the Book of Signs) that Jesus worked and the disciples saw, but they are not recorded in this book. These are recorded so that you may believe (or continue to believe) that Jesus is the Christ, the Son of God, and that believing this you may have life through his name" (Jn 20:30-31).[2]

Mary will be present in both parts of this Gospel and will

witness to faith and to love. She continues to be a model for the life of believers and those who love Jesus as the last Gospel unfolds. Let us now turn to the texts which were given at the beginning of this chapter.

John 1:13

John 1:13 is in the heart of the Prologue of John which introduces the Word of God who pre-exists with God before becoming flesh, that is, taking on our human nature. Though the verse we are considering is translated from the Greek manuscripts as "who were born, not of blood or of the will of the flesh or of the will of man, but of God," there are other ancient manuscripts which are written in Latin and attest to the possibility of an early reading which would suggest the virginal birth of Jesus from Mary: "(He) who was born, not of blood nor of the will of the flesh nor of the will of man, but of God." The ancient witnesses are Irenaeus, Tertullian, Origen, Ambrose, Augustine and Pseudo-Athanasius. Bruce Metzger says, "The singular number may have arisen either from a desire to make the Fourth Gospel allude explicitly to the virgin birth or from the influence of the singular number of the immediately preceding *autou*" (*A Textual Commentary on the New Testament*, p. 197). The most recent study affirming this as the true reading of John is found in Ignace de la Potterie's th rd chapter of his book, *Mary in the Mystery of the Covenant* (pages 96-122).

Other exegetes who have accepted this as the preferred reading are: Harnack, Zahn, Resch, Blass, Loisy, R. Seeburn, Burney, Buchsel, Boismard, Dupont, F.M. Braun, Mollat, J. Galot, and J. McHugh. More recently a doctoral thesis on this verse of the Prologue was published: P. Hofrichter, *Nicht aus Blut sondern Monogen aus Gottgeboren. Textkritische dogmengeschictliche und exegetische Untersuchung zu Joh 1, 13-14*, Würzburg, 1978. The significance of the reading is that the Fourth Gospel would also be attesting to the virgin birth in its Prologue as do Matthew and Luke in their opening chapters. It

must be noted, however, that all of the Greek manuscripts as well as
the majority of patristic texts and versions of this Gospel attest to a
plural reading which emphasizes the faith of all those believing in
Jesus, hence, the plural. Thus on the basis of this overwhelming
testimony the official reading is the plural. At the same time, we
must keep in mind that the text in the singular appears in writers who
are prior to the oldest Greek manuscripts stemming from the fourth
century. Besides its Marian import, there is also a good exercise for
the student in textual criticism in the study of this verse. In the book,
Mary in the New Testament, the authors give some cogent arguments for
reading this text in the plural which would conform more to the
context of the Prologue and also refer to the believers rather than to
the Word being born of a virgin. The authors end their comment
with respect for the great Johannine scholar Sir Edward Hoskyns
who "maintained that the plural was the original reading but
thought that the language was so phrased as to recall the virgin birth
of Jesus" (*MNT*, p. 182).

The plural reading would contrast believers with unbelievers
who are referred to in John 1:11: "He came among his own and his
own did not receive him." This would also fit in with the strong
emphasis on faith in the first part of the Gospel. The Prologue serves
as a hymn to the Word becoming flesh in Jesus; it is also an overture
to the whole Gospel. Verse 11 would attest to those not receiving
the person of Jesus, while verse 12 refers to the fullness of love and
faith commitment: "But as many, however, who did receive him, he
gave them the power to become sons (and daughters) of God, those
who believe in his name...," these are born of God's love (verse 13).
We are then alerted to the themes of faith and love in this Gospel.

John's Gospel, more than the Synoptics, is dominated by these
themes of faith and love. There seems to be little interest in
individual historical questions in the Fourth Gospel.

In taking the traditions about Jesus, the evangelist reflects on
them in light of his faith in the Christ; he then interprets them for
the believers, that is, the readers of this Gospel. John is freer with
the traditional material because of his own theological concerns and
pastoral decisions.

John, however, does focus on the identity of the historical Jesus with the Christ who is Risen (the Christ of faith). With clarity and sharp emphasis he is more interested in the inward approach of personal decision for Jesus through faith and love. Those who are opposed to Jesus manifest the obstacles to such an approach, while the faithful disciples are primarily seen as those who have come to believe in Jesus and, as his friends, are called to a deeper intimacy with him. True understanding of him is only opened through faith in his person which requires a deep insight which bathes both the words and deeds of Jesus in the light of his glorification. J. Schnackenburg states it well:

"A standpoint in regard to the Johannine Jesus can only be taken up existentially, in a personal decision; an encounter with him can only be total, or there can be none at all....

"Moreover, the earthly Jesus is not the Christ who is already exalted with God; this the evangelist knows very well and expresses it clearly in Jesus' anticipation of his *hour*. But this highly significant *hour* of the *lifting up* on the cross shows that his way leads via the cross to God's glory. Because for the believing Church Jesus lives with God, that is, is already the one lifted up, at the same time being present and near to it, the Church should hear the words of the earthly Jesus as the voice of its exalted Lord, of the Christ who is present. And so the evangelist formulates them in majestic language which is very distant from the speech of the synoptic Jesus. A look back to Jesus' earthly ministry and a lifting up of the eyes to the Christ blend with one another; history and present time are joined together in the person of Jesus Christ. Under this aspect, there is for John no diastasis of history and faith" (*Gospel of John*, Vol. 3, p. 390).

The Cana Narrative: John 2:1-12

This is the first of Jesus' seven signs in this Gospel of faith and love. The narrative also offers the first appearance of the Mother of Jesus in this Gospel. Raymond E. Brown sees it as a pericope of incipient Marian meaning;[3] Rudolf Bultmann sees it as reflecting a group favorable to Mary.[4]

The account itself leads to verse 11 which indicates the evangelist's motive for including the incident. This is the beginning of the signs within this Gospel which leads to a revelation about the person of Jesus who primarily is a Revealer of God.

The event of the wedding occurs on the *third day* which actually is the final day of a series of seven that have begun in this Gospel after the Prologue; more specifically after the call of Philip (Jn 1:43).[5] We will also see the importance of the *third day* as a reference to the Resurrection of Jesus at the end of this same Gospel.

The miracle at Cana, or better said, the first of seven such signs in John is a unique sign since it happens before Jesus' public ministry. It is without any parallel in the Synoptics; nor is there a hint of it in the Apocryphal Gospels. Bultmann, and Faure much earlier thought it sprang from a Signs-Source (*Semeia Quelle*) which had a series of miracles or signs from Jesus. It has some family circle reminiscences somewhat like Mark 3:31-35. Interest in this pre-ministry phase of Jesus' life came after the Passion Narrative was well formulated in the Gospels. Our interest in this first of Jesus' signs leads us to pose questions about the pre-Gospel tradition of the Fourth Gospel. Most exegetes work with Faure's and Bultmann's suggestion of a Signs-Source for the provenance of the Cana account. More recently there has been almost total rejection of any theory that would link this to a Dionysian wine symbolism.

The account is a unit in itself (2:1-11) with a short but important transitional verse (2:12). Looking more closely at the narrative there are indications that the event itself has been reworked by the evangelist who gives it a theological meaning for the believing community. This springs from his own reflection on the tradition and sacred memory of this happening. This theological intention was not present in the more primitive account of the miracle itself. Bultmann, McCool, and Brown point this out in their commentaries and studies on Cana. R.T. Fortna, in his study of the Signs-Source has reconstructed it in this manner:

[1]And /.../ there was a wedding in Cana (of Galilee and the
mother of Jesus was there).
[2]Jesus and his disciples were also invited to the wedding
[3]and {they had no wine, for the wine at the wedding gave
out} Jesus' mother said to him /.../
[5]/.../ to the servants, "Do whatever he tells you."
[6]six stone water jars were lying there /.../ filled with two or
three measures
[7]Jesus said to them, "Fill up the jars with water." And they
filled them to the brim.
[8]And he said to them, "Now draw some out and take it to the
chief steward.' So they took it.
[9]When the chief steward tasted the water become wine /.../
he called the bridegroom (the chief steward)
[10]and said to him, "Everyone serves the good wine first, and
the inferior wine after the guests have become drunk.
You have kept the good wine until now."
[11]{This first of his signs he did} Jesus /.../and his disciples
believed in him.[6]

In the perspective of the theology of the Prologue and what
has ensued after John 1:1-18, Cana is a culmination of what has been
witnessed to by the Baptist and what has been revealed to the first
disciples of Jesus.

Certain Christological titles also have appeared in Jesus'
encounters with his disciples. Not only does the evangelist's technique of mentioning the sequence of seven days lead to this
conclusion, but also the unfolding of themes within the context of
the pericope show that the Cana account is essential to the revelation of Jesus. Some of the themes are presented for the first time.
They will be developed as the Gospel moves on toward the uplifting
and glorification of Jesus. Already the reader is alerted to such words
as woman, mother of Jesus, hour, and glory. There are also the
symbols of the water, the wine, the stone jars, the servants, and the
third day.

B. Lindars and R.E. Brown point out that the miracle takes

place in the highlands of Galilee where the Synoptics emphasize that no miracle was worked. From the Apocryphal Gospels we see an analogy with the Cana account for in them Jesus as a child performs prodigies in his family and home setting. In a canonical Gospel, the closest account to Cana would be the narrative of Luke when Jesus is found in Jerusalem in the temple (2:41-51). His knowledge is stupendous, his purpose is to do the will of God. Similarities to Mary at Cana are seen in her pondering over and her pursuing the point thereby eliciting Jesus' negative statement to her, "What concern is this to you and me?" She moves ahead telling the chief steward to "Do whatever he tells you."

Johannine and Lucan redaction are more favorable to Mary than Mark who shows Jesus not placing ultimate value in family ties (Mk 3:31-35). The narrative of Cana also hints at a more favorable image of Mary than that of Mark.

In the canonical Gospel of John, that is, as it is now presented in its final form in the New Testament, the emphasis of Cana is a Christological one, not a Marian one. Jesus is at the center of this story as is seen by verses 11 and 12. There are also possibilities of ecclesial interests such as the Eucharist and Baptism in the scene. Mary is present in the account as a necessary catalyst for the first of the signs of Jesus. In the final great sign, that of the Death and Exaltation of Jesus on the Cross, Mary is again present. There are some parallels in Cana and Calvary in the themes of water, blood, wine, woman, hour, disciple, and mother of Jesus. Yet, Cana can also be studied in itself separate from John 19:25-27 and still present a positive image of Mary.[7]

The intention of the evangelist is a theological one in his use of the Cana event. This is the beginning of the replacements that Jesus will accomplish both through his words, his actions, and his life. Cana begins this series of replacements wherein the rite of Jewish purification symbolized by the six water jars is transformed into a superabundance of wine (120 gallons), great in quality as well as quantity. This symbolizes the overflowing of the Spirit as well as the plenitude of Messianic promises at the Messianic banquet. The community of believers could easily see the Eucharist and Baptism as being intended by the text which the evangelist has presented to them. This replacement theme is a key to almost every transforming scene symbolized by the signs in the first twelve chapters in which the fullness of Jesus' glory and the fulfillment of the *hour* of Jesus' glorification unravels. The theme of *hour* takes in the entire Paschal Mystery of the passion, death, resurrection, and glorification of Jesus.

We turn now to the individual lines of the Cana narrative. John 2:1 follows upon Jesus' promise in 1:50-51 in which Nathanael, who comes from Cana, is told, "You will see greater things than these." And Jesus said to him, "Very truly, I tell you, you will see heaven opened and the angels of God ascending and descending upon the Son of Man." The wedding at Cana then commences and John takes great care to mention: "Jesus did this, the first of his signs, in Cana of Galilee, and revealed his glory; and his disciples believed in him" (Jn 2:11).

Mary, the mother of Jesus, is mentioned immediately and probably is the person who was initially invited. She will be important in the unfolding of this first sign of Jesus more as a catalyst than as an intercessor. Keeping in mind what we have said of the Markan image of Mary (named), we turn to the Johannine one, in which she is four times called by the evangelist, the *mother of Jesus* and *woman* by Jesus. Mary's personal name is not given but the more universal titles of mother and woman are brought forward by evangelist and Jesus respectively.

John 2:3: "They have no wine." The statement implies that Mary has some trust that Jesus could do something about this inconvenience at the wedding party. His own reply seems to show that a burden has been placed upon him by this request. There is misunderstanding on the part of Mary here, but as the scene unfolds matters are clarified. The Johannine Jesus conveys a mysteriousness about who he is and a glimmering of the heavenly reality that is present in this ordinary event.

John 2:4: "Woman, what concern is that to you and me?" In this

Gospel, even though this is the first instance of a son addressing his mother in this manner, there is no negative connotation to the term *woman*. In fact, in other scenes the term is used for the Samaritan, for Mary Magdalene, and then for Mary again at Calvary. The other words are certainly not very affirming, but the encounter with the mother and the son does not stop with them but continues on in the unfolding of the first of Jesus' signs. Mary's role as catalyst is essential to the development of the scene. As in the other signs there may be first a rebuke but once faith enters, the request then is granted. Though she is not called a disciple, she is with those who believe in Jesus through this first of his signs (Jn 2:11-12). Jesus' words can be understood both as a question, "Has not my hour come?" (Vanhoye) or simply as a statement, "My hour has not come." The interpretation of Vanhoye[8] would then lead readers into understanding this as the beginning of the work of Jesus through his suffering, death, resurrection and glorification which is the theological meaning of the term *hour* in later passages in John. There is a definite ambiguity in this verse which enables the reader to ponder, like Mary, the meaning of these words of Jesus.

In almost all of the instances in this Gospel in which a woman is involved, there is a similar rebuke sometimes stronger sometimes more gentle than the one Jesus gives to Mary here. Yet, in each instance the woman comes to believe more deeply in the person of Jesus and she follows through on his word. Before a sign is given, the women are given the challenge of Jesus' words which lead to a deeper faith in him. The pattern we see in Cana is also present in the scene with the Samaritan woman (4:4-42), Martha (11:1-44), and Mary Magdalene (20:11-18). Thus Mary at Cana would be among the women believers who come to do what Jesus is saying, that is, understand him in his call to believe more deeply in him as the Revealer of God.

John 2:5: "Do whatever he tells you." A. Serra[9] sees this as similar to the covenantal response given at the Exodus Event by the people of Israel. Mary, the new Israel, follows with the same "yes" of her people in the new call of Jesus to understand the meaning of his *hour*. This event of a covenantal "yes" happened on a *third day*. R. Garafalo, in his recent doctoral study of Cana, argues for understanding the *third day* not in the light of the Exodus Event but in light of the Resurrection. Perhaps, both are intended by the evangelist. The Exodus Event is the greatest in the history of Israel; the Resurrection is the foundation for all Christian belief.

These last words of Mary in the Gospel, "Do whatever he tells you," show her trust in her son. On a deeper level they certainly confirm a very correct Christology on her part, namely, that Jesus is the one to whom we must turn, not Mary. She is there merely as the agent and catalyst. These words are also found in Genesis 41:55 and are used by Pharaoh to the Egyptians in time of famine. Could Mary be seen as a faithful remnant of Israel pointing to the new economy which will go beyond and transform the first one?

John 2:6-8: The purification of the six water pots of the Jews indicates another Johannine theme, namely, the replacing of the symbolism of Judaism with that of Christianity. John will continue this replacement theme for the Sabbath, the Feast of Lights or the Dedication of the Temple, for the Passover, and for the origins of the Messiah. G. Sloyan notes the importance of Johannine symbolism here: "(The evangelist. . . is more concerned with the implications of the purification requirement for the dusty hands and feet of travelers who are ritual observants: namely, that the water of one epoch — that of the narrative — must be replaced by the wine of another, the age inaugurated by Jesus' words and deeds. In this account the symbolism is everything" (*John*, [*Interpretation Series*], John Knox Press, Atlanta, 1988, p. 35).

Conclusion about Cana as the First Sign

Though the Cana event can be studied in itself, it does offer more possibilities when seen within the entire theology, symbolism, and structure of the Fourth Gospel. From earliest times the patristic reading of both Cana and Calvary were within a Messianic perspective because of the common symbolism found in John 2:1-12 and John 19:25-28a. Terms like *woman* and *hour* are essential to both pericopes. Symbolism flowing from the water to the wine of Cana and the blood and water flowing from Jesus' side immediately after the giving of the Mother of Jesus to the beloved disciple and the disciple to the Mother lead us to such a messianic interpretation. De la Potterie among others has kept alive this patristic interpretation: "An antiphon for Vespers of the Epiphany expresses this so well: 'Today the Church is united to her heavenly Spouse, for... the guests are gladdened by the water changed into wine.' That is the main exegesis of the scene in patristic tradition, but it has been almost completely lost sight of by modern authors. The messianic context of Cana, which is an anticipation of the cross, is already a first indication: the passage at Calvary cannot be read simply at the level of a son's filial duty to his mother. There, too, we are on the *messianic* level" (de la Potterie, *The Hour of Jesus*, Alba House, 1990, p. 108).

That the Cana event took place *on the third day* is another important notion. In the light of other references to the third day, we are led as readers to see a symbolic reference to the Resurrection of Jesus, his greatest sign in this as well as the other Gospels. The wedding also completes the series of seven days enumerated from the beginning of Jesus' call to his disciples, thus a new creation theme or a Christian celebration of the Sabbath in Jesus' Resurrection is possible. Finally, the *hour* of Jesus which is mentioned in John 2:3 is also a possible reference to the Resurrection and exaltation of Jesus.

Another important observation made by de la Potterie is the following: "The Cana story, considered solely from the literary and philological point of view, is not the beginning but the end of a section: after the Prologue, the first section of the Gospel begins with John the Baptist (1:19) and ends at 2:12. This section forms a unit having for its main theme the progressive revelation as Messiah of the unknown man who comes to the Jordan. John says of him: 'I myself did not know him; but for this I came baptizing with water that he might be *revealed* to Israel' (1:31). All the evidence shows that this chapter constitutes an essentially messianic context, given the number of messianic titles it contains. Jesus is the lamb of God who takes away the sins of the world (1:29, 36), the Son of God (1:34, 49), the *Messiah* (1:41), the king of Israel (1:49), the Son of man (1:51). This accumulation of titles culminates in the Cana passage which constitutes its completion and at the same time provides a key to the ultimate interpretation of the entire Fourth Gospel: 'This was the beginning of his signs: he *manifested* his glory' (2:11: the same verb *phaneroun* as for the Baptist at 1:31)" (de la Potterie, *The Hour of Jesus*, pp. 107-108).

The Johannine notion of signs is thus begun in the Cana story and offers the believer an opportunity to grow in faith, which means direct commitment to the person of Jesus with one's whole heart and strength. We learn from the historical or symbolic characters of the Fourth Gospel to go beyond the external sign (the miracle) to the very person of Jesus the Messiah. The Gospel of Signs is thus a Gospel of belief, that is, absolute trust and commitment to Jesus and his words of revelation. In John, the signs are a "partial showing forth of the whole meaning of his ministry, death, and resurrection" (C.K. Barrett, *Peake's Commentary: John*, p. 848).

Other Johannine Texts Referring to Jesus' Origins

John 1:45: Philip found Nathanael and said to him, 'We have found him about whom Moses in the law and also the prophets wrote, Jesus son of Joseph from Nazareth."

John 6:42: They were saying, "Is not this Jesus, the son of Joseph, whose father and mother we know? How can he now say, 'I have come down from heaven'?"

We are aware that John writes on two levels. These two texts illustrate this fact by showing that those who do not know who Jesus really is identify him solely as the "son of Joseph." Once they come to know Jesus through faith then they know him as the only Son of

God. As in Mark, Jesus' only Father is God. In John 5:18 we read: "but (he) was also calling God his own Father, thereby making himself equal to God." In carefully examining the structure of both passages within their context, de la Potterie shows that the evangelist understands the relationship of Jesus to God who is his Father. Joseph is understood to be his father by those who really do not know Jesus through faith. This is never the opinion of the evangelist.

De la Potterie has studied these passages at great length. His conclusion is the following:

"It results then from these two texts that in Galilee Jesus seems to be in reality 'the son of Joseph,' but in no way can one conclude that this is also the conviction of John. Neither the Evangelist nor Jesus himself made use of this formula. In the two passages looked at, this is expressed in the mouth of those who do not know who Jesus is.

" John integrates this opinion of the people into his historical account, but he arranges the structure of his text in such a way that he produces on each occasion a total reversal of the points of view and in the end Jesus is really confessed as 'the Son of God.' For John, that is the true title, the most elevated one for Jesus. J. Willemse writes very judiciously, 'In the mouth of Jesus and that of the Evangelist, the Father of Jesus is always God. There are "others" who speak of Jesus as the "son of Joseph." In John 1:45 it is Philip, in John 6:42 it is the "Jews" '; to speak of Jesus as the son of Joseph, is to pass 'judgments . . . (on him) "according to the flesh" ' " (*Mary in the Mystery of the Covenant*, p. 95).

The Unbelieving Brothers of Jesus: John 7:1-10

This pericope is studied in *Mary in the New Testament* in a balanced manner. Some authors have extended the unbelief of the brothers to Mary, but this is not supported by the texts. The arguments pro and contra are carefully weighed by G. Krodel and K.P. Donfried (*MNT*, pp. 199-201). On one level, some exegetes who work with the literal meaning of the Johannine texts take a negative stance toward the person of Mary in this pericope. Others, who are looking at the theology of the evangelist and at the structure of the Gospel, claim that John may have been aware of the virgin birth (especially in the light of John 1:13 and its variant reading in Latin) as well as the fact that on the literal level John refers to Jesus as the *son of Joseph* in 1:45 and 6:42, but on the theological level and through Johannine irony the texts infer the unique birth of Jesus through Mary. Perhaps, both positions are critiqued by the authors of *Mary in the New Testament* in order to avoid an excess either way, that is, avoiding Marian minimalism and Marian maximalism. We do know that Mary is presented in a very faithful and positive manner in the scene at the foot of the Cross; the brothers of Jesus are not mentioned. To complete the picture of the brothers of Jesus we would have to turn to Luke-Acts, but that is not the method proposed here nor in other exegetical commentaries.

Finally, we may say that John's Gospel is frequently similar to the reminiscences that are found in Mark's Gospel when it comes to this scene of the brothers of Jesus. It is also interesting to note that the miracle of the loaves and fish is found in John, too. It is from this sign/miracle and the revelatory discourse on the Bread of Life that Jesus loses many of his followers. His true disciples remain faithful to him and his word. John says: "For Jesus knew from the first who were the ones that did not believe, and who was the one that would betray him . . . Because of this, many of his disciples turned back and no longer went about with him. So Jesus asked the twelve, 'Do you also wish to go away?' Simon Peter answered him, 'Lord, to whom can we go? You have the words of eternal life. We have come to believe and know that you are the Holy One of God'" (Jn 6:64, 66-69).

The Origins of the Messiah: John 7:41-42, 44

[41]Others said, "This is the Messiah." But some asked, "Surely
the Messiah does not come from Galilee, does he?
[42]Has not the scripture said that the Messiah is descended
from David and comes from Bethlehem, the village
where David lived?". . .
[44]Some of them wanted to arrest him, but no one laid hands
on him.

This passage is easily explained if one accepts the theme of
Johannine irony. The people think they know about Jesus and his
origins, but in reality they do not. Another aspect is that of the
Johannine community which would be in strife with those denying
that Jesus is the Messiah. Certain ecclesial and polemic tones are
present in this passage. We are more in the third stage of Gospel
truth, that is, the time and concerns and theology of the evangelist.
Some exegetes maintain that John is in controversy with other
Christian communities not accepting the high Christology of the
Johannine community looking to Jesus' divine origins rather than
those of the flesh. Hence, whether Jesus is Davidic or not makes no
difference if he is the Son of God or the Word co-eternal with God.
In chapter 7 we are in the geographical confines of Jerusalem in
Judea. Any reference to a Messiah coming from Nazareth would be
spurned, hence the emphasis on Bethlehem for the origins of the
Messiah. Jesus has no success in Jerusalem on the human level, but
it is here that, in the greatest of his signs and at the appointed *hour*,
he will be *lifted up* on the Cross.

John 8:41: "We are not illegitimate children; we have one father, God himself."

These words coming from the Jews who are in hot controversy
with Jesus, may imply polemicism against the Messiah of the
Christians as being illegitimate. This, of course, would be a very

subtle inference. On the literal level it is not justified when seen in the context of John 1:45 and 6:42 where Jesus is known as the son of Joseph. But in the time of the Johannine community the rift between the believers in Jesus and the synagogue leaders had become critical. Such remarks on the part of the participants in both the Synagogue and the Church would have been quite characteristic of the conflict between Jew and Christian after 70 C.E., when rabbinical Judaism consolidated itself at Jamnia. This became a famous center for rabbinic training and for Pharisaism. Between 85 and 130 C.E. there was a curse put on those who were heretics or *minim*. This was brought into the Synagogue Prayer of Eighteen Benedictions. The Johannine believers would be the closest to meriting such a curse from the Jewish believers. "The Johannine community with its proclamation of Jesus as *my Lord and my God* (Jn 20:28) may have been among the first to provoke exclusion by the synagogue authorities, to whom this proclamation would have sounded as if a human being were being elevated to a status that challenged the only *creed* of Israel; 'The Lord our God is one' [Dt 6:4]" (*The New Jerome Biblical Commentary*, 80:24, p. 1344).

Unfortunately, the language of chapter 8 is so vitriolic that it continues to offer problems to the Jewish-Christian Dialogue today. For pastoral reasons it should be carefully explained in our churches. For the historical record it is the earliest Christian text that shows how severe the rift between Judaism and Christianity had come by the year 90 C.E. The Jews could be inferring the illegitimacy of Jesus' origins, while the Christians are saying through this Gospel that the Jews opposing Jesus are children of the devil (Jn 8:44).

We leave these controversial texts of chapters 7 and 8 of John to turn to the most sublime of the Marian texts within the Fourth Gospel, the scene of entrustment of the Mother of Jesus to the Beloved Disciple (Jn 19:25-28a).

The Mother of Jesus at Calvary: John 19:25-28a

[25]Meanwhile, standing near the cross of Jesus were his mother, and his mother's sister, Mary the wife of Clopas, and Mary Magdalene.

[26]When Jesus saw his mother and the disciple whom he loved standing beside her, he said to his mother, "Woman, here is your son."

[27]Then he said to the disciple, "Here is your mother." And from that hour the disciple took her into his own home.

[28]After this, when Jesus knew that all was now finished, he said (in order to fulfill the scripture), "I am thirsty."

Like Cana, the Calvary scene has been treated frequently and at great length by Catholic exegetes, theologians, and spiritual writers. Amidst this we have the most varied of interpretations given to this scene. For one of the significant articles on the earliest commentaries on these verses, we are indebted to Fr. T. Koehler,[10] professor emeritus of the International Marian Research Institute. For the more recent commentaries on the verses we have R.E. Brown, R. Schnackenburg, I. de la Potterie, B. Vawter, and P. Perkins.

These few lines are best understood in their context within the framework of the Passion Narrative of John. This is especially true in the events directly prior to Jesus' death. There has also been some creative insight from scholars who have worked with the structure and parallels of the Fourth Gospel, such as Joseph Grassi,[11] J. Alfaro,[12] M. Girard,[13] and P. Ellis.[14] The creativity of such studies helps the reader to see relationships through the vocabulary, themes, scenes, persons, and theology of the fourth evangelist.

Center stage to Jesus are his Mother and the Beloved Disciple. Is he the son of Zebedee? Is he the witness and first inspired disciple behind the text and sources of the Fourth Gospel? Or is he a symbolic figure of all believers? These are the questions that theologians and exegetes have wrestled with in recent decades. The scene is complicated. It rests on a tradition which differs from that of the Synoptics in the fact that the women and the Beloved Disciple are near the Cross of Jesus, while in Matthew, Mark, and Luke they are looking at the Cross from a distance.

Which tradition is older? Which is more authentic? Did the fourth evangelist take this from a pre-existent source or did he create it himself in the light of the theology of his Gospel? In Mark's Gospel the women are looking at the Cross from afar (Mk 15:40, 47). This is undoubtedly the source for Matthew and Luke. Some of the names given in the Synoptics correspond with those offered by John, but here, they are at the Cross, and standing nearby is Mary, the Mother of Jesus. It is Jesus who in his final moments speaks special words to both the woman who is his mother and the disciple who is beloved. The words are full of meaning and, as is characteristic with the evangelist, may have a deeper sense than the plain literal understanding attached to them in an entrustment of filial concern and piety of Jesus towards his mother.

The Beloved Disciple who is especially revered by this community is more than a recipient who will take Mary to his home. Moreover, the women are contrasted with the soldiers who are also at the Cross and perform the executionary acts for a criminal being crucified on the eve of the great Sabbath of the Passover, just when the lambs would be led to their sacrifice in the temple area. The evangelist has assuredly shaped this traditional material with his own theological intentions. We have in this scene not the words of a final editor, but materials which are carefully planned by the inspired evangelist. R. Schnackenburg attests that "The text as it stands can be understood very well as an offering of the evangelist based on the tradition of the women at the Cross" (*The Gospel According to John*, Vol. 3, New York: Crossroad, 1987, pp. 275-276).

He also links the scene of the seamless garment to the scene at the foot of the Cross. The ecclesial symbolism of the seamless garment was strong in patristic commentaries. In more recent years, some exegetes have also seen such theological symbolism and given it, together with the presence of Mary and the Beloved Disciple at the foot of the Cross, an ecclesial meaning.[15] Was there a double tradition about the women and the Cross only after the death of Jesus as we have in Mark and Matthew? If this is so, then here in John's Gospel they are contrasted with the soldiers and are present as Jesus gives his parting words to those whom he loves, his mother and the Beloved Disciple. We note that in Luke the reference to the women also mentions that they are standing at a distance: "All his friends stood at a distance; so also did the women who had accompanied him from Galilee, and they saw all this happen" (Lk 23:49).

Later traditions tend to become more definitive and particular. In John's Gospel there is a question of how many women are there at the Cross. It ranges from four to two depending on the commentator. Recently, exegetes favor two pairs of women, one unnamed, the other named. The first mentioned are the relatives of Jesus, then follow the two named Mary who are distinguished by additional information. In the Synoptics it is only Mary Magdalene whose name agrees with those mentioned. We may ask about Mary, the wife of Clopas: is she the other Mary mentioned? In Mark 15:40 — "the mother of James the Younger and Joses." In Matthew 27:56 — "the mother of James and Joseph." In Luke 24:10 — "the mother of James." We may ask whether Clopas was a brother of Joseph, the husband of Mary, the mother of Jesus. Eusebius tells us that another son of Clopas, Simeon, was the second overseer of Jerusalem after the death of James, the brother of the Lord (Eusebius, *H.E.* IV. 22. 4). Can this Simeon be identified with the brother of the Lord mentioned in Mark 6:3: "Is not this the carpenter, the son of Mary and brother of James and Joses and Judas and Simon, and are not his sisters here with us?" Just as the names of the twelve tend to get confused the farther down the list, a similar confusion exists in regard to the names of those near Jesus at the Cross and likewise mentioned in connection with his family.

In the more recent studies of this pericope there has been progress in seeing the messianic and ecclesiological meaning of the texts. In the perspective of the entire Gospel, both Cana (2:1-12) and the scene about the seamless garment (19:23-25) are related by theme and vocabulary to our passage. The scene also continues into verse 28 which grammatically is to be joined to the last testament and words of Jesus on the Cross; thus once Mary is entrusted to the Beloved Disciple, then all was finished according to the Scriptures. The fact that Jesus says, "I thirst," is not what is being fulfilled, but the entire life of Jesus which is being lifted up to God after Jesus has spoken to the woman at the foot of the Cross and to the Beloved Disciple.

The first millennium of interpretations of this scene were presented almost exclusively in a moral sense, namely, that Jesus was taking care of his mother by entrusting her to the Beloved Disciple who in turn takes her to his home. With Rupert of Deutz (1080-1130), there is a breakthrough on the interpretation which goes more deeply into Johannine symbolism. It sees Jesus giving Mary as "Synagogue" or "Faithful Daughter of Zion" to the faithful and perfect believer, the Beloved Disciple. It is they who will receive the Spirit of Jesus as he breathes it forth and as blood and water flow from his side. All of these scenes are focused on the central scene of Jesus' last moments with the woman and the Beloved Disciple. More recently R. Bultmann in his commentary on John's Gospel saw Mary as representative of the Jewish people while the Beloved Disciple represented the new followers of Jesus.

The seamless robe is symbolic of the unity that Jesus brings about for the believers. This is the unity of the messianic people who believe in Jesus as Messiah and who come together after their dispersion. As the high priest for that year had prophesied, "Jesus was about to die for the nation, and not for the nation only, but to gather into one the dispersed children of God" (Jn 11:51-52). Jesus also had prayed before his death for this purpose: "that they may be one, as we are one, I in them and you in me, that they may become completely one, so that the world may know that you have sent me and have loved them even as you have loved me" (Jn 17:22-23).

Jesus' death immediately follows our scene and is connected with it through the prepositional phrase *so that* which can be read in this manner according to the philological analysis of C. Bampfylde: "After this, Jesus, knowing that all was accomplished so that the Scripture might be fulfilled, said, 'I thirst.'" Fr. de la Potterie summarizes this succinctly: "The fulfillment of the Scripture was brought about, not by Jesus saying: 'I thirst,' but in the previous episode; there Christ's mission was completed, *tetelestai, consummatum est*. This sentence, therefore, contains two elements which refer back to the scene described in verses 25-27: the first two words: *meta touto*, 'after this,' and also the mention of the fulfillment of Scripture. 'After this' says John, that is to say after the scene he just described, Jesus has accomplished his messianic mission in the way it appears in Scripture. Now all is finished. Jesus has completed his task. Thus his last messianic action has been described in the scene with Mary and the disciple" (de la Potterie, *The Hour of Jesus*, pp. 109-110).

R. Bultmann and I. de la Potterie point out that the verb *tetelestai* (to accomplish, to finish, to bring to an end) is a key word linking this final scene of Calvary with the beginning of the Book of Glory (13:1). In the opening verse of this chapter we read: "Now before the festival of the Passover, Jesus knew that his hour had come to depart from this world and go to the Father. Having loved his own who were in the world, he loved them to the end." *Telos* is the word for *end* but it also can imply that his love for the intimate disciples surrounding him was also a complete and full love for them. This would refer to his great intimate love also for the two who are at the foot of the Cross, Mary and the Beloved Disciple. They would be given to one another, and the Beloved Disciple would take Mary not merely into his home, but especially into his intimacy which he had learned from Jesus. De la Potterie sums it up: "In the Greek we read: *eis telos*, which means at one and the same time: 'to the end' and also 'to the limit.' That is to say: to the last and simultaneously to the highest expression of his love for his own. This final limit of love was realized on the cross, where Jesus could say in all truth: 'It is finished,' it is achieved, the final goal of love has been reached" (*The Hour of Jesus*, p. 110).

Let us now take a closer look at the verses of our pericope.

Verse 25: *Para to stauro tou Iesou* (at the cross of Jesus). This is only found in John's Gospel. This separates Mary from the others who are being identified with the others crucified. This s specifically the Cross of Jesus. It is emphasized in such a way that we have to think of Johannine symbolism indicated in the theme of Jesus *being lifted up* and also in the salvation event that happens because of his crucifixion. In chapter 3 John has Jesus saying, "And just as Moses lifted up the serpent in the wilderness, so must the Son of Man be lifted up, that whoever bel eves in him may have eternal life. For God so loved the world that he gave his only Son, so that everyone who believes in him may not perish but may have eternal life" (Jn 3:14-15). Just as the Passion was predicted three times in the Synoptics, so does John three times use the expression *to be lifted up* as meaning Jesus' exaltation on the Cross (8:28 and 12:32). John 19:25 is also the only place in the New Testament where the dative case with the person is so used that it probably means next to the crucified one. Thus those women and the Beloved Disciple are not mere spectators or bystanders. They are participants in the drama of salvation being enacted upon the Cross.

We may again ask, how many women are meant by John? This depends on how one punctuates the sentence. Jerome in his Vulgate reads three women were present: *"Mater Jesu, eius soror Maria Cleophae, et Maria Magdalene."* Today many exegetes admit four being present: (1) the mother of Jesus, (2) her sister, (3) Mary the wife of Clopas, and (4) Mary Magdalene. In Matthew's parallel which has the women looking on from a distance we read: "Among them were Mary Magdalene, and Mary the mother of James and Joseph, and the mother of the sons of Zebedee" (Mt 27:56).

Verses 26-27 show a pattern which is used by John elsewhere and is indicative of revelation being given. This is called a "revelation schema." It first appears in John 1:26, 36, and 47. This schema contains four parts: (1) two or more persons are present; (2) one notices or sees the other(s); (3) the expression "Look" or "Behold" prefaces a statement about the person(s); (4) there is a title or a word which reveals something about that person. Here, it would refer to

Jesus telling Mary, "*Woman* behold your son"; then to the disciple, "Behold your mother." This would indicate the importance of the title *Woman* being given to Mary at this most solemn moment. The reader already knows that Jesus has called her this at Cana. Now the completion of his *hour* indicates that the Woman who is present is symbolic of something that is revelatory. If it meant the filial piety the disciple showed her, this would be only the moral interpretation of the scene. If it means that she is the Woman to be welcomed intimately into the belief and love of the disciple, then there may be the beginnings of a community of faith represented in this mutual entrustment. Mary as a type of the Synagogue and as the Daughter of Zion is received by the believing disciple into his own heart and home. The parallelism — "Woman, behold your son . . . Son, behold your mother" — shows there is more to this declaration of Jesus than a filial concern for his mother. Mary alone is given the special title *Woman* which is indicative of a role she will have in the future. She is addressed first by Jesus. She is given the principal place in this last testament of Jesus. It is Mary who stands next to the Crucified Jesus while the disciple stands next to Mary.

Is the Beloved Disciple a historical person? From the evidence of the Gospel he is the original witness who believes in Jesus and continues to do so to the very end. He is also a type and symbol for all believers just as Nicodemus and the Samaritan woman were symbolic of a faith that grew once they discovered who Jesus is. This disciple whom Jesus loves was presented already in 13:23: "One of his disciples, the one whom Jesus loved, was reclining next to him." He also appears in the final redaction of the Fourth Gospel, that is, in chapter 21. There we read: "That disciple whom Jesus loved said to Peter, 'It is the Lord'" (Jn 21:7). And in verse 20: "Peter turned and saw the disciple whom Jesus loved following them; he was the one who had reclined next to Jesus at the supper and had said, 'Lord, who is it that is going to betray you?'" The great intimacy with Jesus that we spoke of is certainly essential to the life of the Beloved Disciple. In each reference there is singular manifestation of this intimate relationship with Jesus. He is the disciple who is the object of the love of Jesus. Thus he is a type and model for all disciples of Jesus.

Given to Mary at the foot of the Cross, this disciple is the symbol for all the faithful believing in the crucified Jesus. Jesus confides him to Mary as mother of this disciple. All believers, men and women, are the brothers and sisters of this disciple who welcome Mary as mother. They also realize that Jesus has accomplished the will of the Father in heaven. The disciple and Mary are to carry on this mission of Jesus as the community of Jesus and the community of the Beloved Disciple and the Mother.

The fourth evangelist has repeatedly spoken of Mary as the mother of Jesus in this Gospel. The word "mother" is mentioned on eleven occasions, and only in the Nicodemus dialogue does it refer to someone other than Mary. In all of these references she is the mother of Jesus; now at Calvary, she becomes mother of the disciple who represents all of Jesus' followers, all of his future brothers and sisters.

Sir Edward Hoskyns, the great Johannine scholar of the last century, in commenting on verse 27 says: "The union of the beloved disciple with the Mother of the Lord is the prefiguring and image of the charity of God's Church" (*The Fourth Gospel*, London: Faber, 1947, p. 530).

More recently, J. Grassi says, "As a remembering mother and carrier of tradition, Jesus' mother is the preeminent witness of who Jesus is, how Jesus died, and the effects of his death. The first and seventh signs (Jn 2:1-12 and Jn 19:25-27) carry the common elements of the presence of Jesus' mother, the centrality of the *hour*, and the focus on obedience as well as the interconnection of water/wine/spirit" (*Catholic Biblical Quarterly*, 48, 1986, p. 80).

These are the spiritual realities of the testament of Jesus from the Cross. These are what are fulfilled in the Scriptures. For here as at Cana, Mary is called *Woman*, that unusual title given to her by Jesus. The evangelist has not used her personal name Mary so that she is considered not as an individual person but as the Woman to whom a special gift and special role have been entrusted. If there was a certain negative tone at Cana, this was to push aside the physical relationship she shared with Jesus and to lead her to the deeper faith commitment to his person. Now that the *hour* has come in its fullest at the seventh sign, she and the Beloved Disciple are persons of Jesus' complete love. They represent all of Jesus' brothers and sisters who are there and who will come into the community of believers. Mary is symbolic of this community as its mother. Her deeper spiritual motherhood begins at the foot of the Cross as Jesus accomplishes all. The victory is now complete. The prince of darkness is vanquished (cf. Gn 3:15; Rv 12). She is, together with the Beloved Disciple, a companion to her Son in this ultimate victory over death, sin, and Satan.

The fullness of Jesus' life is received by the Woman and the Beloved Disciple standing beneath the Cross. Mary and the Beloved Disciple represent all Christians as they look upon Jesus and believe. Then, as they receive his Spirit in the flowing of the blood and water, the community begins. The Church is brought forth from the Cross and the life-giving water which flows from the side of Christ (Baptism) and his blood (Eucharist). These two disciples are symbols of the call to perfect discipleship which reaches its highest demands in the context of a believing community and in the love and care they have for one another. Mary, in this Gospel, is always in the center of the community, either that of Israel at Cana or that of the Church which is begun on Calvary. Intimacy, love, and mutual sharing are presented at the *event* at the foot of the Cross. Discipleship and belief in Jesus as the Messiah and the Revealer of God began at Cana through the *sign* of water made into wine, while at Calvary *sign* becomes *event* in the continuing of the love Jesus had for the disciple and his mother now being theirs to share with each other. . . . "But to all who received him, who believed in his name, he gave power to become children of God" (Jn 1:12).

Endnotes

1. Bertrand Buby, S.M., "The Commitment of Faith and Love in the Fourth Gospel," *Review for Religious*, Vol. 40, No. 4, 1981, pp. 561-567.

2. George MacRae, S.J., *Invitation to John* (Garden City, New York: Image, 1978), p. 226.

3. Raymond E. Brown, *The Gospel According to John I-XII*, Vol. 29 (Garden City, New York; Doubleday, 1966), pp. 97-111.

4. Rudolf Bultmann, *The Gospel of John* (Philadelphia, Pennsylvania: Westminster, 1971), pp. 113-121; 671-673.

5. Richard J. Dillon, "Wisdom Tradition and Sacramental Retrospect in the Cana Account (Jn 2,1-11)," *Catholic Biblical Quarterly* 24 (1962) pp. 268-96.

6. R. T. Fortna, *The Gospel of Signs* (Cambridge, UK: Cambridge University Press, 1970).

7. Robert Garafalo, "History, Theology and Symbol: The Mother of Jesus in the Cana Narrative, 1950-1990," International Marian Research Institute, Dayton, 1993 (unpublished thesis).

8. Albert Vanhoye, S.J., "Interrogation et éxegèse de Cana (Jn. 2,4)," *Bibilica* 60 (1974), pp. 157-167.

9. Aristide Serra, *E C'era la Madre di Gesù...saggi di esegesi biblico-mariana* (1978-1988), (Milano: Cens, 1989), pp. 490-494.

10. Theodore Koehler, S.M., "Les principales interprétations de Jn. 19,25-27, pendant les douzes premiers siècles," *Etudes Mariales* 16 (1959), pp. 119-155.

11. Joseph Grassi, "The Role of Jesus' Mother in John's Gospel: A Reappraisal," *Catholic Biblical Quarterly* 48, 1986, pp. 67-90.

12. Juan Alfaro, "The Mariology of the Fourth Gospel," *Biblical Theological Bulletin*, Vol. X, 1980, no. 1, pp. 3-16.

13. Marc Girard, "La composition structurelle des sept signes dans le quatrième évangile," *Studies in Religion/Science Religieuse* 9, 3 (1980), pp. 315-324.

14. Peter Ellis, *The Genius of John: A Composition-Critical Commentary on the Fourth Gospel* (Collegeville: Liturgical, 1984).

15. Charles Kingsley Barrett, *The Gospel According to John* (Philadelphia, Westminster, 1978), pp. 458-459.

Chapter Six

THE VISION OF THE APOCALYPSE:
A WOMAN CLOTHED WITH THE SUN:
Revelation 11:15-12:17

In order to place the vision of a Woman clothed with the sun and having the moon beneath her feet, I have situated the scene within its larger context. It depicts the seventh angel blowing his trumpet, hence, the completion of another great moment in the vision of John the Elder. The text is clear in its Messianic message:

15Then the seventh angel blew his trumpet, and there were loud voices in heaven, saying,

> 'The kingdom of the world
> has become the kingdom of our Lord
> and of his Messiah,
> and he will reign forever and ever.'

16Then the twenty-four elders who sit on their thrones before God fell on their faces and worshipped God,
17 singing,

> 'We give you thanks, Lord God Almighty,
> who are and who were,
> for you have taken your great power
> and begun to reign.
18The nations raged,
> but your wrath has come,

and the time for judging the dead,
for rewarding your servants, and the prophets
and saints and all who fear your name,
both small and great,
and for destroying those who destroy the earth.'
¹⁹Then God's temple in heaven was opened, and the ark of
his covenant was seen within his temple; and there
were flashes of lightning, rumblings, peals of thunder,
an earthquake, and heavy hail.

In this scene both judgment and salvation are announced. In
the light of what follows in the vision of the Woman, we are led to
see that the ultimate eschatological victory of the Messiah lies
ahead in the future, but, at the same time, the death of Jesus upon
the Cross is the real victory over all forces of evil. Somewhat like the
combination of the realized and yet future eschatology of the
Gospel of John, the Book of Revelation looks back to the death of
Jesus and from that event shows the ultimate victory over all sin and
death. The eschatology of the Apocalypse is more elusive because
of the colorful and dramatic symbolism the seer uses. The first cycle
of visions, with the seven seals and the seven trumpets, depicts all
of the woes, judgments, and ultimate salvation. Here the number
seven shows the completeness of the vision and its meaning.

It is the final verse of the scene that leads to the section on the
Woman clothed with the sun. Verse 19 above is the revelation of
God through the ark of the covenant. This symbol is carried over
from the Hebrew Scriptures into the new revelation after the one
who has been pierced is celebrated on the Lord's day, Sunday (cf. Rv
1:7, 10). This revelation of God above in the ark of the covenant is
now complemented by the vision of the Woman representing those
who faithfully follow the true witness of God, Jesus the Messiah. In
chapter 21 the Woman will be the symbol of the new Jerusalem, the
heavenly bride. Here she is united with God and those who are
children of God through the covenant promise: "I will be their God
and they will be my children" (Rv 21:7). It is helpful to remember

that the visions blend and complement each other. The seven seals and the seven trumpets and perhaps any mention of seven helps to unite the seer's visionary experiences. It is now in chapter 12 that the vision of the Woman and the Dragon happens:

[1]A great portent appeared in heaven: a woman clothed with the sun, with the moon under her feet, and on her head a crown of twelve stars.
[2]She was pregnant and was crying out in birthpangs, in the agony of giving birth.
[3]Then another portent appeared in the heaven: a great red dragon, with seven heads and ten horns, and seven diadems on his heads.
[4]His tail swept down a third of the stars of heaven and threw them to the earth. Then the dragon stood before the woman who was about to bear a child, so that he might devour her child as soon as it was born.
[5]And she gave birth to a son, a male child, who is to rule all the nations with a rod of iron. But her child was snatched away and taken to God and to his throne;
[6]and the woman fled into the wilderness, where she has a place prepared by God, so that there she can be nourished for one thousand two hundred sixty days.
[7]And war broke out in heaven; Michael and his angels fought against the dragon. The dragon and his angels fought back,
[8]but they were defeated, and there was no longer any place for them in heaven.
[9]The great dragon was thrown down, that ancient serpent, who is called the Devil and Satan, the deceiver of the whole world — he was thrown down to the earth, and his angels were thrown down with him.
[10]Then I heard a loud voice in heaven, proclaiming,
'Now have come the salvation and the power and the kingdom of our God, and the authority of his Messiah, for the accuser of our comrades has been thrown

down, who accuses them day and night before our
God.

[11]But they have conquered him by the blood of the Lamb
and by the word of their testimony,
for they did not cling to life even in the face of death.

[12]Rejoice then, you heavens and those who dwell in them!
But woe to the earth and the sea, for the Devil has
come down to you with great wrath, because he
knows his time is short!'

[13]So when the dragon saw that he had been thrown down to
earth, he pursued the woman who had given birth to
the male child.

[14]But the woman was given the two wings of the great eagle,
so that she could fly from the serpent into the wilderness, to her place where she is nourished for a time,
and times, and half a time.

[15]Then from his mouth the serpent poured water like a river
after the woman, to sweep her away with the flood.

[16]But the earth came to the help of the woman; it opened its
mouth and swallowed the river that the dragon had
poured from his mouth.

[17]Then the dragon was angry with the woman, and went off
to make war on the rest of her children, those who
keep the commandments of God and hold the testimony of Jesus.

[18]Then the dragon took his stand on the sand of the sea-
shore.

Adela Yarbro Collins, one of the excellent commentators on
the Book of Revelation, states: "This chapter (12) is not a unitary
composition, but is based on two sources: a narrative describing the
conflict between a woman with child and a dragon (reflected in vv.
1-6 and 13-17), and a narrative depicting a battle in heaven (vv. 7-
9). It is probable that these sources were composed by non-
Christian Jews and that John edited them, making numerous additions, including the hymn of vv. 10-12" (*New Jerome Biblical Commentary*, 63:43, p. 1008).

Recently, E. Corsini's commentary on the Apocalypse offers a new approach to interpreting the Old Testament references and symbols in the light of the Paschal Mysteries of Jesus.[1] Corsini noted that Origen employed the Apocalypse to interpret the Fourth Gospel. Origen did this by using the Paschal Mystery as the key towards understanding the Book of Revelation. This helps us to balance the excessive eschatological interpretation that has been given to this book by the greatest event of Jesus, his Resurrection from the dead after his death upon the Cross. We must remember that the seer's vision on the island of Patmos starts on a Sunday, "the Lord's Day" (*en te Kuriake hemera*: Rv 1:10). The magnificent Christological titles in the first eight lines are certainly part of the immediate context that led Corsini to see an emphasis on the Paschal Mysteries. This interpretation will help us to see Mary within the Paschal Mysteries especially in the scene of the Woman clothed with the sun.

Within Catholic tradition there are two interpretations given to the twelfth chapter of Revelation. One sees in the Woman the image of the Church; the other the image of Mary, the mother of the Messiah. Some exegetes see only one aspect of this scene, namely, the ecclesial; others, only the Marian interpretation. Just as we pointed out the necessity of seeing the paschal as well as the eschatological message of the Book of Revelation, so, too, in the Church's tradition there is both an ecclesial interpretation and a Marian accommodation of the text. During the patristic period and throughout the first millennium the ecclesiological interpretation was foremost; in the Middle Ages a Marian interpretation prevailed. Since we are in the realm of apocalyptic and symbolic language, care must be taken not to be rigid in the interpretation relying only on the historical-critical method. Archetypal language has a universal character about it and individuals are touched by it in ways that a narrative language cannot accomplish. We can also see the profound religious experiences of visionaries, seers, and those caught up in the climate of reported apparitions. Many are led to conver-

sion. There are several outlines given for the Book of Revelation.
One which is simple and helpful is the following:

1. Chapters 1 to 3 are the Introduction with the revelation of
   the Son of Man to the seer, the elder John.
2. Chapters 4 to 11 are the revelation of the Paschal Mystery
   through the symbol of the Lamb slain but now alive before
   the throne of God. The Lamb alone opens the seven seals
   one by one. The prayers of the saints hasten the coming of
   the "Great Day" and the trumpets are sounded.
3. Chapters 12 to 22 are definitely dedicated to the progress
   and development of the Church during the time of persecution and oppression till the time of the final victory in the
   heavenly Jerusalem.
4. Finally, the Epilogue (Rv 22:6-21) is a dialogue between the
   Messiah and his bride, the Church: "My return is near...
   Oh, yes, come, Lord Jesus!"

Our ecclesial and Marian section is found in the second part
of the book beginning with chapter 12, but each symbol and vision
is part of a whole and is better understood and experienced when
seen and read within the context of the entire book.

First Interpretation: The Woman as a Symbol of the Church

In the prophetic and apocalyptic literature of the Hebrew
Scriptures the symbol of *woman* is often associated with Israel, that
is, with the People of God. This symbol has been taken from its
Hebrew source and now is applied in the Book of Revelation to the
People of God known now as the Church. This encompasses those
who believe Jesus is the Messiah who has redeemed his people by
his death and Resurrection. John McHugh describes the symbol:
"The woman clothed with the sun is (...) the archetypal symbol of
the indestructible Church, of the eternal Church" (*The Mother of Jesus*

in the New Testament, p. 467, 281-282). This Woman is also identified with the "Daughter of Zion," another symbol taken over from the prophetic writings and used to describe the Church in the New Testament. The people of the earth who follow the Woman and who pass through many sufferings and persecutions with her will ultimately share in the victory of the Lamb and in the joy of the Messianic Wedding of the Lamb.

André Feuillet has shown how the description of the New Jerusalem found in Isaiah mirrors the description of the Woman clothed with the sun in Revelation.[2] He also makes use of the Canticle of Canticles to show similar symbolism for the Woman who is the Mother of the Messiah and the Bride of the Lamb. Here are the two passages from Isaiah:

> Arise, shine; for your light has come, and the glory of the Lord has risen upon you....

> The sun shall no longer be your light by day, nor for brightness shall the moon give light to you by night; but the Lord will be your everlasting light, and your God will be your glory. Your sun shall no more go down, or your moon withdraw itself; for the Lord will be your everlasting light, and your days of mourning shall be ended. Your people shall all be righteous; they shall possess the land forever. They are the shoot that I planted, the work of my hands, so that I might be glorified (Is 60:1, 19-21).

In Revelation 21:23 we see that a similar symbolism is present which shows everything is to be for the glory of God: "And the city has no need of sun or moon to shine on it, for the glory of God is its light, and its lamp is the Lamb."

The Song of Songs also seems to fit the background for the Woman: "Who is this that looks forth like the dawn, fair as the moon, bright as the sun, terrible as an army with banners?" (Sg 6:10).

The image of the Woman clothed with the sun and the moon beneath her feet and with twelve stars surrounding her head is to be explained through the use of such symbolism within the Hebrew Scriptures. The light of the sun and the sun itself is used for the glory of God. Christ is also called the Light. The Woman who represents the Church is thus wrapped in God's glory.

The moon, though mysterious, peaceful, and beautiful, also receives all of its light from the sun. The twelve stars symbolize perfection or completion. There is also the importance of the twelve tribes of Israel and the twelve apostles. The Church is the new Israel; the apostles are the foundation pillars of the Church. J. McHugh says, "It is not only the Church of history, but the people of God predestined to become the city of God" (*The Mother of Jesus in the New Testament*, p. 464).

We notice the paradox or contrast in the situation of the Woman being clothed in splendor with the sun and then described as being pursued, oppressed, and persecuted. In the Book of Revelation the sacred liturgy combines the heavenly and the earthly, eternal time with past time. Christ as the Alpha and Omega embraces both in the Book of Revelation. The same Woman clothed with the sun is also the Woman in the pangs of childbirth as well as the one pursued by the Dragon or the Devil. This is a symbol of the eschatological sufferings of the Daughter of Zion and of the Church. The prophet Micah provides us with the source for such symbolism:

"Writhe and groan, O daughter Zion, like a woman in labor; for now you shall go forth from the city and camp in the open country; you shall go to Babylon. There you shall be rescued, there the Lord will redeem you from the hands of your enemies" (Mi 4:10).

Another passage which is a key to the symbolism used in the twelfth chapter of Revelation is a messianic one from Trito-Isaiah:

[6]Listen, an uproar from the city! A voice from the Temple! The voice of the Lord dealing retribution to his enemies!
[7]Before she was in labor she gave birth; before her pain came upon her she delivered a son.
[8]Who has heard of such a thing? Who has seen such things?

Shall a land be born in one day? Shall a nation be
delivered in one moment? Yet as soon as Zion was in
labor she delivered her children.
⁹Shall I open the womb and not deliver? says the Lord; shall
I, the one who delivers, shut the womb? says your
God.
¹⁰Rejoice with Jerusalem, and be glad for her, all you who
love her; rejoice with her in joy, all you who mourn
over her — that you may nurse and be satisfied from
her consoling breast; that you may drink deeply with
delight from her glorious bosom (Is 66:6-11).

Corsini and Feuillet see the mystery of the Church and that of
Mary respectively bound up with the Paschal Mystery of Jesus' own
suffering and death which is also compared with the labor pains of
a woman. In John 16:21-22 we see this symbolism:
"When a woman is in labor, she has pain, because her hour has
come. But when her child is born, she no longer remembers the
anguish because of the joy of having brought a human being into the
world. So you have pain now; but I will see you again, and your
hearts will rejoice, and no one will take your joy from you."
If the vision of the seer of Patmos is experienced as the
heavenly liturgy being celebrated on the Lord's Day, a positive and
non-threatening message comes through the symbolism described
by the author. Time and eternity mesh because of the ever effective
salvific event of Jesus' death and Resurrection. *Kairos* not *chronos* is
lived out through the vision and the faith of those listening or
reading the Book of Revelation. This offsets the bizarre dramatiza-
tion and terrifying interpretation given to this book by movies and
over-zealous latter-day prophets. The Paschal Mystery balances
the eschatological and apocalyptic if we read the symbols in this
manner. The whole book then becomes a vision of the Church
throughout the ages even though it is historically written within the
context of Domitian's persecution. The victory of the Lamb and the
assured safety of the Woman (the Church) are the message for that
time and for the present.
It is not the messianic and historical birth of Christ in the

Infancy Narratives of Matthew and Luke, but the new birth that begins on Easter Sunday. In the New Testament the Resurrection is described several times as a new birth. Both in the Acts of the Apostles and in the Epistle to the Hebrews we see this attested:

> [32]And we bring you the good news that what God promised to our ancestors
> [33]he has fulfilled for us, their children, by raising Jesus; as also it is written in the second psalm: "You are my Son; today I have begotten you" (Ac 13:32-33).

And in the Epistle to the Hebrews the same psalm is used to refer to Jesus' superiority over the angels: "For to which of the angels did God ever say, 'You are my Son; today I have begotten you'?" (Heb 1:5).

The symbolism of computing time also springs from Daniel 7:25 and 12:7 in which we can figure out that the time is a period of three and a half years or twelve hundred and sixty days. This is the time in which the Woman flees to the desert for protection. Again the symbolism of the desert comes forth which takes on the aspect of a place of solitude and safety prepared for the Woman by God. This symbolism is found in Hosea and in the Psalms. De la Potterie captures this symbolism:

> The desert was then the place where Israel had retired and where it had been very specially protected and guided by God. It is certain that the aspect of safeguard and of protection is specially underlined in the greater number of accounts of the happenings which took place in the desert. Let us recall, for example, the beautiful passage of the life of the prophet Elijah (1 K 19:4-16): he fled before his persecutors, stayed alone in the desert near Horeb — the mountain where Moses also had his meeting with God — and received there his mission in a poignant experience of God. The desert is, then, a

place of protection and of defense against dangers and enemies, but it is also a privileged place of encounter with God (*Mary in the Mystery of the Covenant*, p. 255).

The Dragon is the symbol of the ancient serpent of Genesis 3 and also the symbol for the Devil or Satan. Scholars of different schools of thought have seen the possibility of Genesis 3:15 forming the background for the writer of the Apocalypse. There we read: "I will put enmity between you and the woman, and between your offspring and hers; he will strike your head, and you will strike his heel." The vision explains the source of evil which is personified as the Dragon. The believers are those who identify themselves with the Woman and make efforts to protect her. The Dragon's attack symbolizes their experience of hardship, alienation from the dominant cultural values, and, for some, arrest, punishment, and even execution. The identification of the Dragon with Satan implies that their hardships are not meaningless, random events; rather, they result from a systematic and universal tension between order and chaos, good and evil.

From the above reflections we can easily see how the Woman represents the new Israel or the Church. Now we come to a more difficult question. Is Mary, the Mother of Jesus, symbolically depicted in chapter 12 of the Book of Revelation? From those who espouse the historical-critical method, the symbolism of Mary seems to be eisegesis rather than exegesis. Revelation is seen as a work written to address a Christian community undergoing intense persecution at the end of the first century. Irenaeus gives a foundation for the historical interpretation: "The Revelation was seen not long ago, but almost in our generation, at the end of Domitian's reign" (*Adversus Haereses* 5.30, 3). Domitian was often seen by the Christians as a *Nero redivivus* (cf. *Mary in the New Testament*, p. 225, n. 495).

These critics state the writing is highly symbolic and apocalyptic and has to be studied from similar literary works in order to have the keys to its interpretation. It suited the psychological and political context of the people who were in need of reassurance, strengthening, warning, and direction in how to find meaning in what they were enduring. Their faith and the hearkening back to such symbolism helped them achieve this assurance.

From the religious imagery embedded in the Hebrew Scriptures, the Woman is a symbol for both the Old and the New Israel. The former has brought forth the Messiah who has now been taken up to God's throne as the Lamb; the latter, the Church, still experiences both persecution and the sustaining providence of God:

"So when the dragon saw that he had been thrown down to the earth, he pursued the woman who had given birth to the male child. But the woman was given the two wings of the great eagle, so that she could fly from the serpent into the wilderness, to her place where she is nourished for a time, and times, and half a time" (Rv 12:13-14).

Sources for such imagery flow from the canonical and inspired Scriptures (e.g., Gn 3:15; 6:1-4) as well as from the Dead Sea literature (esp. 1 QH, III, 7-10 and 1 Qap Gen 21:13) and from apocryphal works (I Enoch 6-19, Jubilees 5; Adam and Eve 12-17). The central section regarding the fall of the angels is derived from Jewish sources:

> [7]And war broke out in heaven; Michael and his angels fought against the dragon. The dragon and his angels fought back,
> [8]but they were defeated, and there was no longer any place for them in heaven.
> [9]The great dragon was thrown down, that ancient serpent, who is called the Devil and Satan, the deceiver of the whole world — he was thrown down to the earth, and his angels were thrown down with him (Rv 12:7-9).

Jesus refers to this in Luke's Gospel, "I watched Satan fall from heaven like a flash of lightning" (Lk 10:18). Michael is listed as the highest of the angels together with Gabriel. For this reason they are called archangels. To Michael belonged the privilege of being the official representative of God. His name in Hebrew means "Who is like God." He and Gabriel were special protectors of Israel and it is they who led Israel into freedom. Rabbinic literature links Michael and Gabriel with the Angel of God who appeared to Moses in Exodus 3:2. Rabbi Johannan (d. 279 C.E.) said, "It was Michael." Rabbi Chanina (circa 225 C.E.) said, "It was Gabriel... In general, where Michael appears, there indeed was the Glory of the Shekinah" (*Kommentar zum Neuen Testament aus Talmud und Midrasch*, by Strack-Billerbeck, p. 814). It is in a court scene that Michael defends Israel against Sammael (Satan).

Undoubtedly, the latter Jewish commentaries also go back to the battle between Michael and Satan. Within the Jewish literature there is also a reference to Mount Zion where Michael will triumph. This could account for the writer of the Apocalypse linking this section with the Woman clothed with the sun, who is also considered to be the Daughter of Zion (see Strack-Billerbeck, op. cit., p. 812).

The Marian Interpretation of the Vision

There is a Marian interpretation given to this passage by many Catholic scholars, especially A. Feuillet. Though the symbolism is used in a collective representation of the Church and the Messiah, there are designations which can logically lead one to see the child of the Woman as Jesus Christ the Messiah. From other New Testament sources we know that his Mother is Mary of Nazareth. This, of course, would be a deduction which goes beyond the literal meaning of the text of Revelation, but when one is working with symbolic language many possibilities and alternative interpretations arise. Above, we alluded to the Daughter of Zion as being a further designation of the Woman (see 4 Esdras 9:38-10:55). Mary, too, is often seen by New Testament scholars such as Laurentin, Lyonnet, Deiss, Koehler, and Feuillet as the Daughter of Zion.[3]

Within the Catholic Tradition the passage is easily accommodated to Mary both from the context and background of Revelation 12 as well as from a more dramatic and liturgical reading of the text. In fact, this text is used for the Feast of the Assumption. Mary as woman represents Israel in its origins and its development.

The birth of the Messiah is bound up with the limitations of human nature, namely, being born of a human mother. Mary then from her very unique historical situation can also be the source for an archetypal symbol of the Woman who is Israel (original) and the Church (developed). As archetype of the Church she is a sign that the Church is surrounded by God's power and protection ("clothed with the sun"). She also is in continuity with the original people of God, yet she is also a sign for the renewed people of God, the Church. The stars above her head apply to both the twelve patriarchs of the tribes of Israel, and the twelve apostles. As Israel was led into the desert where God nourishes her with manna and bears her up on eagle's wings (Dt 32:10-11), so, too, is the Church protected by God.

Since the scene is symbolic, it can be interpreted by methods other than the historical-critical method. I would suggest that the method of structural exegesis combined with the semiotic method be used to gain insights into this symbolism. The text lends itself to the following topographical "square":

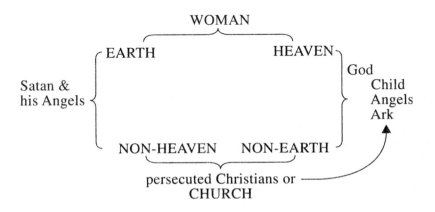

The Woman appears in the heavenly area but is hidden on earth. She spans both a heavenly and an earthly reality. She is on the side of the heavenly reality that includes the divine court, the ark, the child and God's angels. There is an echo of David's going up to Jerusalem with the ark, ard Mary going to Ain Karem to visit her cousin Elizabeth. The ark is a symbol of God's presence.

The Dragon is opposite all this as opposed to God. The Dragon is excluded from heaven. The angels of Satan are non-heaven, that is, they are out of the sphere of goodness and are totally in the realm where evil is enacted. The persecuted Christians are non-earth because they are children of the Woman in the heavens where their true homeland and inheritance is; they have, however, not yet achieved heaven and so they are "non-heaven." They are related to the Woman but are not totally protected from the rage of the Dragon. The Woman, an archetype of the Church, looks to her final fulfillment of glory in God once the Dragon is defeated and persecution of her offspring ceases.

With more reflection on the part of the reader a deeper symbolic structure emerges:

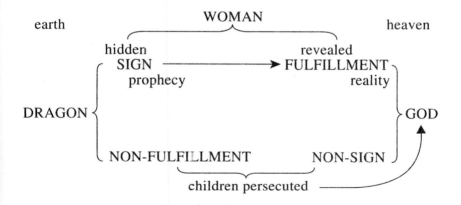

Here *sign* carries with it the meaning of the "already" but "not yet," the partially revealed and limited reality and the ultimate fulfillment and victory of God. The Church comes into its inheritance as the new Jerusalem that already has begun. God who is truth and who is always faithful already has won the battle and has kept the promise made to the children of God. The divine fullness of reality is present already in heaven where the heavenly court is moving on toward final triumph through the salvation of those who were being persecuted. The Dragon is also a sign but is symbolic of non-fulfillment, ultimate defeat and deception for all who believe and accept its rule or succumb to the threats of persecution. Siding with the forces of evil, untruth, chaos, disorder, and injustice lead to ultimate frustration and non-fulfillment. The children of the Woman experience hardships only for a short time in their suffering persecution from the Dragon. They are not a sign any more than God is, but they will, through his saving victory, enter into fulfillment which is in the heavenly Jerusalem in its final triumph over all that is evil, deceptive, and rebellious.

Contemporary exegesis places the scene of the Woman in an ecclesiological context both historically and symbolically. Is there a possibility of synthesizing the ecclesial interpretation with those exegetes who see a Marian dimension in Revelation 12? If we only had the verses of the Apocalypse, it would be difficult to see a Marian interpretation because there is no evidence of a virginal birth for the Woman nor is she named. The symbol is more a collective one of the Church and God and the Messiah.

Within the Bible the title Daughter of Zion occurs in the prophetic texts and in the Psalms. This image for Jerusalem is also an image of the Church in its emergence and in its tradition. Mary, too, is a personification of the Daughter of Zion despite the paradoxical nature of this biblical title. Mary is also the Woman in the Fourth Gospel who is present at the foot of the Cross and to whom the Beloved Disciple is given. Many exegetes have seen an ecclesial image in this Woman at the foot of the Cross. It is here, within a Johannine tradition that we can see the possibility of merging both the collective and the personal through the texts. Gerhoh of Reichersberg (1093-1169 C.E.) states that "From the Church which is holy, Mary was the first beginning."[4] Thus the theme of the Woman in Revelation seen primarily as Church can also be seen in the light of the other episodes of the New Testament in which Mary is called Woman. A. Feuillet affirms:

"In John 19:25-27 three traits characterize the Mother of Jesus which are not found in the other Gospels... (1) The insistence with which the Mother of Jesus is called 'Woman.' The coincidence in this regard between the two scenes of Cana and Calvary betrays an intention which ought to be of doctrinal import. In particular... it is that she is Woman in some manner par excellence that Mary is given as mother to St. John; (2) she has, then, other children besides Jesus, for the Savior himself gives his beloved disciple to Mary as her son; (3) this spiritual maternity is united to Golgotha...

"These traits characterized likewise the Mother of the Messiah in the Apocalypse. She also is called Woman... She also has other children besides the Messiah; finally, to her is also attributed a metaphorical childbirth which is united to the Cross... It becomes certain that we are in the presence, once more, of an authentic Johannine tradition common to the Gospel and to the Apocalypse" (A. Feuillet, "Le Messie et sa Mère", 303-304 in *Révue biblique* 1959, 58-86 and in *Études johanniques*, Desclée de Brouwer, 1962, 273-310).

St. Ambrose (339-397 C.E.), who is an excellent commentator on the Scriptures, already saw this synthesis: "May the Christ from the height of the cross say also to each of you: 'There is your mother.' May he say also to the Church: 'There is your son.' Then we will begin to be children of the Church when we see Christ triumphant on the cross" (St. Ambrose. *In Lucam VII*, 5 [*PL* 15, 1787]).

The Johannine scholar, I. de la Potterie has this to say: "It is the text of John 19:25-27 which has made possible the Marian interpretation of Revelation 12. There is, however, a difference between the two pericopes. If the two visions are not identical they are, however, perfectly complementary.

"In the Fourth Gospel especially at Cana, but also near to the cross, the accent is placed on the individual person of Mary, the Mother of Jesus (it is thus that John names her), but with the ecclesiological resonances which we have tried to echo.

"In Revelation 12 the relationship of who Mary personifies is reversed. Here in the foreground is the ecclesiological aspect: the Woman Zion, the Church, will become the Spouse of the Lamb in the definitive conclusion of the Covenant (21:1-9). This indeed concerns the Church, but more precisely inasmuch as she is the accomplishment of what from the beginning had already been realized in the figure of Mary. In Revelation 12 the accent falls on the Church, but with Mariological resonances. These are two approaches which are complementary, in a constant dialectic between two aspects (individual and collective) of the same mystery, that of the covenant of the daughter of Zion with God" (*Mary in the Mystery of the Covenant*, p. 263).

Summary and Conclusion to Revelation 12

For understanding the Book of Revelation, it is necessary to discover the historical period and the community climate and sociology in which and for which the book was written. Since so much has been perpetrated and foisted on this great symbolic book in the name of prophecy and predictions about the Second Coming of Christ (the Parousia), it is even more mandatory that scholars and spiritual writers offset the propaganda and sensationalism that make use even of Scripture. This is especially true in the United States where not only literature and preaching but also the film industry has exploited the Book of Revelation. Just to mention a few of such films: "The Omen," "Damien," "The Final Conflict," "The Seventh Sign," "The Rapture." Hal Lindsey's *The Late Great Planet Earth* sold more copies than any other work of non-fiction when it came out, making him perhaps the best selling author of the seventies. Normally these sensational approaches to Revelation center on the Beast and the number 666 (Rv 13:18) which continue to inspire and generate ingenious solutions ranging from their being applied to a Pope by anti-Catholic propaganda, to Hitler, Stalin, or Henry Kissinger! Others with overblown excitement and panic through their homespun eschatologies say that the number 666 applies to the products of the People's Republic of China or even the U.S.A., since 666 is supposedly their product code. Some people have even moved to "deserted places" to await the "Rapture."

It is through the historical-critical method that some of the above aberrations can be corrected. To provide a balanced approach to any section of the Book of Revelation we have to direct our attention to the world that is behind the text. This is the real world that we must discover. This is the proper way of looking at things disclosed by the text. It is this world which is the link between the immediate past of the author and that of the present reader or commentator. The text always presents or proposes a world of its own which has its own structure, its own symbolism, its own coherence, and a capacity to generate audiences of its own.

Adela Yarbro Collins offers similar insights: "I would agree that full explanatory power should not be given to the author's intention. What the writer intended to say and what he or she actually said may not always coincide. By being committed to writing and being preserved and circulated beyond its original situation, a text is, in a certain sense, cut loose from the existential, historical situation in which it emerged. When we read Paul's first letter to the Corinthians, we do not know what he had said to them orally on visits that predated the letter, and we do not have immediate access to their shared assumptions. But we can attempt to reconstruct these things as hypotheses and judge which are more and which are less likely If we do not engage in such historical reconstruction, we may fail to understand or may misunderstand the text" (*Crisis and Catharsis,* p. 19).

E.D. Hirsch argues that the meaning of a text must be linked to the situation in which it emerged. Interpretations that do not take the original historical context seriously express the significance of the text to various readers, but cannot claim to express its normative meaning or range of meanings.

In going back to the first interpreters of the Book of Revelation we can say that Papias, the bishop of Hierapolis (not far from Laodicea) was the first Christian to mention this book in his writings. Laodicea was one of the towns to which the book is addressed.

Andreas of Caesarea, who wrote a commentary on this book in the sixth century, says that Papias knew the book and considered it to be divinely inspired and commented on at least one of its passages.

Justin the Martyr, who resided for a time at Ephesus, another of the seven cities of the Apocalypse, says in his dialogue with Trypho that the Book of Revelation was written by the Apostle John.

Irenaeus of Lyon attributes both the Gospel of John and the Book of Revelation to John the son of Zebedee. Hippolytus, Tertullian, and Origen apparently followed Irenaeus in their judgments about the authorship of this book.

Jerome and much later Martin Luther saw little value in this book and let it be known in their own acerbic styles.

In all of these apologists and writers we find a morsel of the truth, but also a cornucopia of conjecture.

Again the words of A. Collins sum up what we can say about the history of these early commentators:

"Irenaeus' opinion that the Gospel and the Apocalypse were written by the same person is untenable. Historical-critical scholarship has marshalled a great deal of evidence against the presupposition. Some excellent arguments against common authorship were already put forward by Dionysius, bishop of Alexandria in Egypt in the second half of the third century. He was led to examine the issue because he, as an allegorist in the manner of Origen, who inclined towards spiritual interpretations, was critical of a movement in a neighboring region that involved an earthly messianic reign of a thousand years, characterized, for example, by an abundance of wine. This is the same kind of millennnarianism that Cerinthus apparently held. Unlike the Alogi and Gaius, Dionysius did not claim that Revelation was pseudonymous. He claimed that he did not wish to set it aside, since it was so highly esteemed by many in the Church. He did, however, raise doubts about its authority. Dionysius assumed that the Gospel was indeed by John the son of Zebedee and argued that both works could not be. Thus, he concluded, Revelation must be by some other man by the same name John. In spite of Dionysius' statement that the Apocalypse was by a holy and inspired man, it lost influence in the East. Its sacred status was disputed officially until Athanasius supported its inclusion among the sacred books in 367 C.E." (*Crisis and Catharsis*, p. 31).

For our own study we saw that the image of the Woman is what is of interest to us. Yet, the text points to the destiny of that Woman as being what is important. The story is told to help the readers understand and respond to their own situation of oppression and persecution with the hope and ultimate victory promised by this scene. We can see in the Woman a number of possible interpretations:

1. She is Israel (the Daughter of Zion), the nation from whom the Messiah comes (cf. Is 66:7-8). Israel awaits the birth of the Messiah in that text. Our writer, a Jewish Christian, "christens" the passages and pictures that depict Israel.

2. The Woman is the Church or the developed and fulfilled Israel who like the original Israel is the mother of all those faithful to God.

3. Medieval expositors and pastors and some contemporary exegetes and Mariologists see Mary as the Woman and model of the Church in this scene. Mary is the daughter of Zion — the quintessential expression of the old Israel as the community of faith and obedience, awaiting the coming of the Messiah, the community in which the Messiah is born. She is also the quintessential expression of the new Israel, of those who 'believe' and are justified on the

grounds of their faith, of those who obey his word and who suffer for the testimony of Jesus (cf. de la Potterie, *Mary in the Mystery of the Covenant*, pp. 239-264; *Revelation: A New Catholic Commentary on Holy Scripture*, (New York: Nelson, p. 1277).

Exegetical Remarks on Revelation 12:1-17

v. 1: The Woman is a felicitous sign for the believing community for she appears in the highest heaven while sin occurs in the abyss or the lowest regions.

She is the antithesis of the Harlot, and as a symbol is as figurative and important in Revelation as the Lamb.

In Codex A she is not looking at the sun but is clothed with it. The sun, perhaps representing God, is a rampart or protection around the Woman who represents the community or Church.

v. 2: *en gastri echousa* (being with child) is a phrase that is used of Mary in Matthew 1:18, 23. Being in birth pangs (*basanizome*) is also found in John 16:19-22 and Isaiah 66:7. The birth symbolized is something more than a physical birth.

v. 3: The Dragon, being fiery red, is a symbol of murder and persecution. The Mishnah sees the Dragon as the work of idolatry. Our author identifies it with the Devil and the Serpent of old.

v. 4: "Sweep" signifies the colossal size of this sea monster.

v. 5: There is no reference to the virginity of the Woman or to her son as the firstborn.

v. 14: "A time and times and half a time" refers to 42 months in 12:6 (42 = 3 1/2 x 12). We are led to think of Matthew's similar use in his genealogy, 3 x 14 generations. There were 42 symbolic generations before the coming of the Messiah; there would be 42 more till his return again.

v. 17: Only this text and Genesis 3:15 put such great emphasis on the seed or offspring of the Woman.

All of the symbolism used in this scene: the sun, the moon, the stars suggest that our Woman is the community of Israel as seen in Exodus 19:5-6: "Now therefore, if you obey my voice and keep my covenant, you shall be my treasured possession out of all the peoples. Indeed, the whole earth is mine, but you shall be for me a priestly kingdom and a holy nation." The scene is also suggested by the twelve tribes portrayed in Revelation 7.

Anther source is Isaiah 26:17-27:1, especially for Revelation 20:1-4. This biblical background suggests that the Woman portrays faithful Jerusalem; that she suffers, but will receive help from God; that her opponent is the Dragon. Dupont-Sommer applies the oracles of Second Isaiah to the mother of the Messiah (Isaiah 52:13-53:12 = the Suffering Servant Oracles).

There are also some parallels with the Qumran document of 1QH 3: "In the light of the OT texts and I QH 3 it seems reasonable for the Woman to be the faithful priestly and prophetic community, the child a prominent leader, and the Dragon, Satan. Revelation 17-18 mention the harlot, which may be another version of the mother of the asp, the faithless community allied with the fallen angel" (Massingbyrd Ford, *Revelation. The Anchor Bible*, p. 205).

Endnotes

1. Eugenio Corsini, *The Apocalypse: the Perennial Revelation of Jesus Christ*, translated by F.J. Moloney, S.D.B., (Wilmington, Delaware: Michael Glazier, 1983), esp. pp. 17-21.

2. André Feuillet, *Johannine Studies* Staten Island, NY: Alba House, 1965, pp. 275-276.

3. Nunzio Lemmo, "Maria, 'Figlia di Sion,' a partire da Lc 1,26-38, Bilancio esegetico dal 1939 al 1982," *Marianum* 45 (1983) pp. 175-258. This doctoral dissertation contains an excellent bibliography on the topic of the Daughter of Zion, while listing all the Catholic and Protestant scholars who have written on this title. The more complete bibliography is contained in the thesis (cf. No. 37 Pontificia Facultas Teologica Marianum, Roma, 1985).

4. *Lib. de gloria et honore filii hominis*, X, in *PL* 194, 1105A.

Letter from the Congregation for Catholic Education
Rome, 25 March 1988

THE VIRGIN MARY IN INTELLECTUAL AND SPIRITUAL FORMATION

Introduction

1. The Second Extraordinary Assembly of the Synod of Bishops which was held in 1985 for "the celebration, verification and promotion of Vatican Council II"[1] affirmed that "special attention must be paid to the four major Constitutions of the council"[2] in order to implement a programme "having as its object a new, more extensive and deeper knowledge and reception of the Council."[3]

On his part, His Holiness Pope John Paul II has explained that the Marian Year is meant "to promote a new and more careful reading of what the Council said about the Blessed Virgin Mary, Mother of God, in the mystery of Christ and of the Church."[4]

In the light of these developments the Congregation for Catholic Education addresses this present Circular Letter to theological faculties, to seminaries and to other centers of ecclesiastical studies in order to offer some reflections on the Blessed Virgin and to emphasize that the promotion of knowledge, research and piety with regard to Mary of Nazareth is not to be restricted to the Marian Year, but must be permanent since the exemplary value and the mission of the Virgin are permanent. The Mother of the Lord is a "datum of divine Revelation" and a "maternal presence" always operative in the life of the Church.[5]

I. The Virgin Mary: An Essential Datum of the Faith and the Life of The Church

The wealth of Marian doctrine

2. The history of dogma and theology bears witness to the Church's faith about, and constant attention to, the Virgin Mary and to her mission in the history of salvation. Such attention is already evident in some of the New Testament writings and in a number of pages by authors in the sub-apostolic age.

The first symbols of the faith and, successively, the dogmatic formulas of the Councils of Constantinople (381), of Ephesus (431) and of Chalcedon (451) are evidence of the developing appreciation of the mystery of Christ, true God and true man, and at the same time of the progressive discovery of the role of Mary in the mystery of the Incarnation, a discovery which led to the dogmatic definition of Mary's divine and virginal motherhood.

The attention of the Church to Mary of Nazareth runs through the centuries, with many pronouncements about her being made. Without underestimating the blossoming which Mariological reflection produced in earlier periods of history, here we draw only on the more recent.

3. We recall the doctrinal importance of the dogmatic Bull *Ineffabilis Deus* (8 December 1854) of Pius IX, the Apostolic Constitution *Munificentissimus Deus* (1 November 1950) of Pius XII, and the dogmatic Constitution *Lumen Gentium* (21 November 1964), chapter VIII of which is the fullest and most authoritative synthesis of Catholic doctrine about the Mother of the Lord ever to have been compiled by an ecumenical council. Also to be remembered for their theological and pastoral significance are other documents such as *Professio Fidei* (30 June 1968), the Apostolic Exhortation *Signum Magnum* (13 May 1967) and *Marialis Cultus* (2 February 1974) of Paul

VI, as well as the Encyclical *Redemptoris Mater* (25 March 1987) of John Paul II.

4. It is also important to remember the influence of several "movements" which in several ways and from various points of view raised interest in the person of the Virgin and considerably influenced the composition of the Constitution *Lumen Gentium*: the biblical movement, which underlined the primary importance of the Sacred Scriptures for a presentation of the role of the Mother of the Lord, truly consonant with the revealed Word; the patristic movement, which put Mariology in contact with the thought of the Fathers of the Church so that its roots in Tradition could be more deeply appreciated; the ecclesiological movement, which contributed abundantly to the reconsideration and deepening appreciation of the relationship between Mary and the Church; the missionary movement, which progressively discovered the value of Mary of Nazareth, the first to be evangelized (cf. Lk 1:26-38) and the first evangelizer (cf. Lk 1:39-45), fount of inspiration in her commitment to the spreading of the Good News; the liturgical movement, which initiated a rich and rigorous study of the various liturgies and was able to document the way the rites of the Church testified to a heartfelt veneration towards Mary, the "ever-Virgin, Mother of Jesus Christ, our Lord and God";[6] the ecumenical movement, which called for a more exact understanding of the person of the Virgin in the sources of Revelation, identifying more exactly the theological basis of Marian piety.

The Marian teaching of Vatican II

5. The importance of chapter VIII of *Lumen Gentium* lies in the value of its doctrinal synthesis and in its formulation of doctrine about the Blessed Virgin in the context of the mystery of Christ and of the Church. In this way the Council:

— allied itself to the patristic tradition which gives a privileged place to the history of salvation in every theological tract;

— stressed that the Mother of the Lord is not a peripheral figure in our faith and in the panorama of theology; rather, she, through her intimate participation in the history of salvation, "in a certain way unites and mirrors within herself the central truths of the faith";[7]

— formulated a common vision for the different positions about the way in which Marian matters are to be treated.

A. In relation to the Mystery of Christ

6. According to the doctrine of the Council, the relationship between Mary and God the Father derives from her role in relation to Christ. "When the time had fully come, God sent forth his Son, born of a woman... so that we might receive adoption as sons" (Gal 4:4-5).[8] Mary, therefore, who, by her condition, was the Handmaid of the Lord (cf. Lk 1.38, 48), "received the Word of God in her heart and in her body, and gave Life to the world", becoming by grace "Mother of God."[9] In view of this unique mission, God the Father preserved her from original sin, enriched her with an abundance of heavenly gifts and, in the plan of his Wisdom, "willed that the consent of the predestined mother should precede the Incarnation."[10]

7. The Council, explaining the participation of Mary in the history of salvation, expounded, first of all, the multiple aspects of the relationship between the Virgin and Christ:

— she is "the most excellent *fruit* of the redemption,"[11] having been "redeemed in an especially sublime manner by reason of the merits of her Son";[12] thus the Fathers of the Church, the Liturgy and the Magisterium have called her "daughter of her Son"[13] in the order of grace;

— she is the *mother*, who, accepting with faith the message of the Angel, conceived the Son of God in his human nature in her virginal womb through the action of the Holy Spirit and without the intervention of man; she brought him to birth, she fed him, tended him and educated him;[14]

— she is the faithful *handmaid* who "devoted herself totally... to the person and work of her Son, serving under him and with him, the mystery of redemption";[15]

— she is the *cooperatrix* with the Redeemer: "She conceived, brought forth and nourished Christ. She presented him to the Father in the Temple, and was united with him in suffering as he died on the cross. In an utterly singular way she cooperated by her obedience, faith, hope and burning charity in the Saviour's work of restoring supernatural life to souls";[16]

— she is the *disciple* who, during the preaching of Christ, "received his praise when, in extolling a kingdom beyond the calculations of flesh and blood, he declared blessed (cf. Mk 3:35; Lk 11:27-28) those who heard and kept the word of God, as she was faithfully doing (cf. Lk 2:19, 51)."[17]

8. The relationship between Mary and the Holy Spirit is also to be seen in the light of Christ: "she is, at it were, fashioned and formed into a new creature"[18] by the Holy Spirit, and, in a special way, is his temple; [19] through the power of the same Spirit (cf. Lk 1:35) she conceived in her virginal womb and gave Jesus Christ to the world.[20] During the Visitation the gifts of the Messiah flowed through her: the outpouring of the Holy Spirit on Elizabeth, the joy of the future Precursor (cf. Lk 1:41).

Full of faith in the promise of the Son (cf. Lk 24:49) the Virgin is present, praying in the midst of the community of disciples: persevering with them in one accord, we see Mary "prayerfully imploring the gift of the Spirit, who had already overshadowed her in the Annunciation."[21]

B. *In relation to the mystery of the Church*

9. For Christ, and therefore also for the Church, God willed and predestined the Virgin from all eternity. Mary of Nazareth is:

— "hailed as a preeminent and altogether singular *member* of

the Church"[22] because of the gifts of grace which adorn her and because of the place she occupies in the mystical Body;
— *mother* of the Church, since she is Mother of him who, from the first moment of the Incarnation in her virginal womb, unites to himself as Head his Mystical Body which is the Church;[23]
— *figure* of the Church, being virgin, spouse and mother, for the Church is virgin because its fidelity is whole and pure, spouse by its union with Christ, mother of the innumerable children of God;[24]
— virtuous *model* of the Church, which is inspired by her in the exercise of faith, hope and charity [25] and in apostolic work;[26]
— through her manifold acts of intercession, continuing to obtain the gifts of eternal salvation for the Church. By her maternal charity she cares for the brethren of her Son on their pilgrim way. Therefore the Blessed Virgin is invoked by the Church with the titles of *Advocate, Auxiliatrix, Adjutrix* and *Mediatrix*;[27]
— assumed body and soul into heaven, "the *eschatological image* and first flowering" of the Church[28] which sees and admires in her "that which she herself wholly desires and hopes to be,"[29] finding in Mary "a sign of sure hope and solace."[30]

Post-Conciliar Marian developments

10. During the years immediately following the Council, work by the Holy See, by many episcopal conferences, and by famous scholars, illustrating the teaching of the Council and responding to the problems that were emerging gradually, gave a new relevance and vigor to reflection on the Mother of the Lord.

The Apostolic Exhortation *Marialis Cultus* and the Encyclical *Redemptoris Mater* have made a particular contribution to this Mariological reawakening.

This is not the place to list completely all the various sectors of post-conciliar reflection on Mary. However it seems useful to illustrate some of them in summary as example and stimulus to further research.

11. Biblical exegesis has opened new frontiers for Mariology, ever dedicating more attention to the inter-testamental literature. Some texts of the Old Testament, and especially the New Testament parts of Luke and Matthew on the infancy of Jesus and the Johannine pericopes, have been the object of continuous and deep study, the results of which have reinforced the biblical basis of Mariology and considerably enriched its themes.

12. In the field of dogmatic theology, the study of Mariology has contributed in the post-conciliar debate to a more suitable illustration of dogmas brought about in: the discussions on original sin (dogma of the Immaculate Conception), on the Incarnation of the Word (dogma of the virginal conception of Christ, dogma of the divine maternity), on grace and freedom (doctrine of the cooperation of Mary in the work of salvation), on the ultimate destiny of man (dogma of the Assumption). This has required critical study of the historical circumstances in which these dogmas were defined, and of the language in which they were formulated, understanding them in the light of the insights of biblical exegesis, of a more rigorous understanding of Tradition, of the questions raised by the human sciences and with a refutation of unfounded objections.

13. The study of Mariology has taken great interest in the problems connected with devotion to the Blessed Virgin. There has been research into the historical roots of the devotion,[31] study of its doctrinal foundation, of its place in the "one Christian devotion,"[32] evaluation of its liturgical expression and its multiple manifestations of popular piety, and a deepening appreciation of their mutual relationship.

14. Mariology has also been especially considered in the field of ecumenism. With regard to the Churches of the Christian East, John Paul II has underlined "how profoundly the Catholic Church, the Orthodox Church and the ancient Churches of the East feel

united by love and praise of the Theotokos";[33] on his part, Dimitrios I, the Ecumenical Patriarch, has noted that "our two sister Churches have maintained throughout the centuries unextinguished the flame of devotion to the most venerated person of the all-holy Mother of God,"[34] and he went on to say that "the subject of Mariology should occupy a central position in the theological dialogue between our Churches . . . for the full establishment of our ecclesial communion."[35]

With regard to the Reformation Churches, the post-conciliar period has been characterized by dialogue and by the thrust towards mutual understanding. This has brought an end to the centuries-old mistrust, and has led to a better knowledge of respective doctrinal positions; it has also led to a number of common initiatives in research. Thus, at least in some cases, it has been possible to understand both the dangers in "obscuring" the person of Mary in ecclesial life, and also the necessity of holding to the data of Revelation.[36]

During these years, in the area of inter-religious discourse, Mariology has studied Judaism, source of the "Daughter of Sion." It has also studied Islam, in which Mary is venerated as holy Mother of Christ.

15. Post-conciliar Mariology has given renewed attention to anthropology. The Popes have repeatedly presented Mary of Nazareth as the supreme expression of human freedom in the cooperation of man with God, who "in the sublime event of the Incarnation of his Son, entrusted himself to the ministry, the free and active ministry of a woman."[37]

In the convergence of the data of faith and the data of the anthropological sciences, when these turn their attention to Mary of Nazareth, one understands more clearly that the Virgin is both the highest historical realization of the Gospel[38] and the woman who, through her self-control, her sense of responsibility, her openness to others and to the spirit of service, her strength and her love, is the most completely realized on the human level.

For example, the necessity has been noted:

— of drawing out the relevance of the human reality of the Virgin to people in our own time, stressing the fact that she is an historical person, a humble Jewish girl;

— of showing forth the permanent and universal human values of Mary in such a way that discourse about her throws light on discourse about man.

In this context, the subject of "Mary and women" has been treated many times, but it is susceptible of many different approaches, and it is a long way from being exhausted and from yielding its finest fruits; and it awaits further developments.

16. New themes and treatments from new points of view have emerged in post-conciliar Mariology; the relationship between the Holy Spirit and Mary; the problem of inculturation of Marian doctrine and forms of Marian piety; the value of the *via pulchritudinis* for advancing in knowledge of Mary and the capacity of the Virgin to stimulate the highest expressions of literature and art; the discovery of the significance of Mary in relation to some urgent pastoral needs in our time (pro-life, the option for the poor, the proclamation of the Word...); the revaluation of the "Marian dimension of the life of a disciple of Christ."[39]

The Encyclical "Redemptoris Mater" of John Paul II

17. In the wake of *Lumen Gentium* and of the magisterial documents which followed the Council comes the Encyclical *Redemptoris Mater* of John Paul II, which confirms the Christological and ecclesiological approach to Mariology that clearly reveals the wide range of its contents.

Through a prolonged meditation on the exclamation of Elizabeth, "Blessed is she who believed" (Lk 1:45) the Holy Father thoroughly studies the multiple aspects of the "heroic faith" of the Virgin, which he considers "a kind of key which unlocks for us the innermost reality of Mary,"[40] and he illustrates the "maternal presence" of the Virgin in the pilgrimage of faith according to two lines of thought, one theological, the other pastoral and spiritual:

— the Virgin was actively present in the life of the Church —
at its beginning (the mystery of the Incarnation), in its
being set up (the mystery of Cana and of the Cross) and in
its manifestation (the mystery of Pentecost) — she is an
"active presence" throughout the Church's history, being "at
the center of the pilgrim Church,"[41] performing a multiple
function: of cooperation in the birth of the faithful in the
life of grace, of exemplarity in the following of Christ, of
"maternal mediation";[42]

— the deed by which Christ entrusted the disciple to the
Mother and the Mother to the disciple (cf. Jn 19:25-27) has
established the very closest relationship between Mary and
the Church. The will of the Lord has been to assign a
"Marian note" to the physiognomy of the Church, its
pilgrimage, its pastoral activity; and in the spiritual life of
each disciple, says the Holy Father, a "Marian dimension" is
inherent.[43]

Redemptoris Mater as a whole can be considered the Encyclical
of the "maternal and active presence" of Mary in the life of the
Church:[44] in the pilgrimage of faith, in the worship of the Lord, in
the work of evangelization, in progressive configuration to Christ,
in ecumenical endeavor.

The contribution of Mariology to theological research

18. The history of theology shows that an understanding of
the mystery of the Virgin contributes to a more profound understanding of the mystery of Christ, of the Church and of the vocation
of man.[45] Similarly, the close link of the Virgin with Christ, with the
Church and with humanity means that the truth about Christ, the
Church and man throws light on the truth about Mary of Nazareth.

19. In Mary in fact "everything is relative to Christ."[46] In
consequence, "only in the mystery of Christ is her mystery fully
made clear."[47] The more the Church deepens her appreciation of the
mystery of Christ, the more it understands the singular dignity of

the Mother of the Lord and her role in the history of salvation. But, in a certain measure, the contrary is also true: the Church, through Mary, that "exceptional witness to the mystery of Christ,"[48] has deepened its understanding of the mystery of the kenosis of the "Son of God" (Lk 3:38; cf. Ph 2:58) who became in Mary "Son of Adam" (Lk 3:38), and has recognized more clearly the historical roots of the 'Son of David" (cf. Lk 1:32), his place among the Hebrew people, his membership in the 'poor of Yahweh."

20. Everything about Mary — privileges, mission, destiny — is also intrinsically referable to the mystery of the Church. In the measure in which the mystery of the Church is understood the more distinctly does the mystery of Mary become apparent. Contemplating Mary, the Church recognizes its origins, its intimate nature, its mission of grace, its destiny to glory, and the pilgrimage of faith which it must follow.[49]

21. Finally, in Mary everything is referable to the human race, in all times and all places. She has a universal and permanent value. She is "our true sister,"[50] and "because she belongs to the offspring of Adam she is one with all human beings in their need for salvation,"[51] Mary does not disappoint the expectations of contemporary man. Because she is the "perfect follower of Christ"[52] and the woman most completely realized as a person, she is a perennial source of fruitful inspiration.

For the disciples of the Lord the Virgin is a great symbol: a person who achieves the most intimate aspirations of her intellect, of her will and of her heart, being open through Christ in the Spirit to the transcendence of God in filial dedication, taking root in history through hardworking service of others.

As Paul VI wrote, "Contemplated in the episodes of the Gospels and in the reality which she already possesses in the City of God, the Blessed Virgin Mary offers a calm vision and a reassuring word to modern man, torn as he often is between anguish and hope, defeated by the sense of his own limitations and assailed by limitless aspirations, troubled in his mind and divided in his heart, uncertain before the riddle of death, oppressed by loneliness while yearning for fellowship, a prey to boredom and disgust. She shows forth the victory of hope over anguish, of fellowship over solitude, of peace over anxiety, of joy and beauty over boredom and disgust, of eternal visions over earthly ones, of life over death."[53]

22. "Among all believers she is like a 'mirror' in which are reflected in the most profound and limpid way 'the mighty works of God' (Ac 2:11)"[54] which theology has the task of illustrating. The dignity and importance of Mariology, therefore, derive from the dignity and importance of Christology, from the value of ecclesiology and pneumatology, from the meaning of supernatural anthropology and from eschatology: Mariology is closely connected with these tracts.

II. The Virgin Mary in Intellectual and Spiritual Formation

Research in Mariology

23. The data expounded in the first part of this Letter show that Mariology is alive and active in relevant questions in matters doctrinal and pastoral. However it is necessary that the study of Mariology, together with attention to the pastoral problems which are emerging gradually, attend to rigorous research, conducted according to scientific criteria.

24. The words of the Council apply: "Sacred theology rests on the written word of God, together with sacred Tradition, as its primary and perpetual foundation. By scrutinizing in the light of faith all truth stored up in the mystery of Christ, theology is most powerfully strengthened and constantly rejuvenated by that word."[55] The study of the sacred Scriptures, therefore, must be the soul of Mariology.[56]

25. Further, the study of Tradition is essential to research in Mariology because, as Vatican II teaches, "sacred Tradition and sacred Scripture form one sacred deposit of the word of God, which

is committed to the Church."[57] The study of Tradition shows how particularly fruitful in quality and quantity is the Marian patrimony of the various Liturgies and of the Fathers of the Church.

26. Research into Scripture and Tradition, conducted according to the most fruitful methods and with the most reliable instruments of critical enquiry, must be guided by the Magisterium since "the task of authentically interpreting the word of God, whether written or handed on, has been entrusted exclusively to the living teaching office of the Church."[58] This research must also integrate and be strengthened by the more secure fruits of learning in anthropology and the human sciences.

The teaching of Mariology

27. Considering the importance of the Virgin in the history of salvation and in the life of the People of God, and after promptings of Vatican Council II and of the Popes, it would be unthinkable that the teaching of Mariology be obscured today: it is necessary therefore that it be given its just place in seminaries and theological faculties.

28. Such teaching, consisting of a "systematic treatment," will be:

a) *organic,* that is, inserted adequately in the programme of studies of the theological curriculum;

b) *complete,* so that the person of the Virgin be considered in the whole history of salvation, that is, in her relation to God; to Christ, the Word incarnate, Saviour and Mediator; to the Holy Spirit, the Sanctifier and Giver of life; to the Church, sacrament of salvation; to man — in his origins and his development in the life of grace, and his destiny to glory;

c) *suited* to the various types of institution (centers of religious culture, seminaries, theological faculties . . .) and to the level of the students: future priests and teachers of

Mariology, animators of Marian piety in the dioceses, those who are responsible for formation in the religious life, catechists, those who give conferences, and the many who want to deepen their knowledge of Mary.

29. Teaching thus given will avoid one-sided presentations of the figure and mission of Mary, presentations which are detrimental to the whole vision of her mystery. Sound teaching will be a stimulus to deep research — in seminaries and through the writing of licence and doctoral theses — into the sources of Revelation and the documents. Mariological study can also profit from interdisciplinary teaching.

30. It is necessary, therefore, that every center of theological study — according to its proper physiognomy — plan that in its *Ratio studiorum* the teaching of Mariology be included, having the characteristics listed above; and, consequently, with the teachers of Mariology being properly qualified.

31. With regard to this latter point, we would draw attention to the Norms of the Apostolic Constitution *Sapientia Christiana* which provide for licences and doctorates in theology, specializing in Mariology.[59]

Mariology and pastoral service

32. Like every other theological discipline, Mariology has a precious contribution to make to pastoral life. *Marialis Cultus* affirms that "devotion to the Blessed Virgin, subordinated to worship of the divine Saviour and in connection with it, also has great pastoral effectiveness and constitutes a force for renewing Christian living."[60] Also, Mariology is called to make its contribution to the work of evangelization.[61]

33. Mariological research, teaching and pastoral service tend to the promotion of the authentic Marian piety which should characterize the life of every Christian, especially those who are

dedicated to theological studies and who are preparing for the priesthood.

The Congregation for Catholic Education draws the attention of seminary educators to the necessity of promoting an authentic Marian piety among seminarians who will one day be principal workers in the pastoral life of the Church.

Vatican II, treating the necessity of seminarians having a profound spiritual life, recommended that seminarians "should love and honor the most Blessed Virgin Mary, who was given as a mother to his disciple by Christ Jesus as he hung dying on the cross."[62]

For its part, this Congregation, conforming to the thought of the Council, has underlined many times the value of Marian piety in the formation of seminarians:

— in the *Ratio fundamentalis institutionis sacerdotalis* the Congregation requests the seminarian "to have a fervent love for the Virgin Mary, Mother of Christ, who was in a special way associated with the work of Redemption."[63]

— in the *circular letter concerning some of the more urgent aspects of spiritual formation in seminaries* the Congregation noted that "there is nothing better than true devotion to Mary, conceived as an ever more complete following of her example, to introduce one to the joy of believing,"[64] which is so important for anyone who will spend the rest of his life in the continual exercise of faith.

Conclusion

The *Code of Canon Law*, treating of the formation of candidates for the priesthood, recommends devotion to the Blessed Virgin Mary so that, nourished by the exercises of piety, the students may acquire the spirit of prayer and be strengthened in their vocation.[65]

34. With this Letter the Congregation for Catholic Education wishes to reaffirm the necessity of furnishing seminarians and

students of all centers of ecclesiastical studies with Mariological formation which embraces study, devotion and lifestyle. They must:

a) acquire a *complete and exact knowledge* of the doctrine of the Church about the Virgin Mary which enables them to distinguish between true and false devotion, and to distinguish authentic doctrine from its deformations arising from excess or neglect; and above all which discloses to them the way to understand and to contemplate the supreme beauty of the glorious Mother of Christ;

b) nourish an *authentic love* for the Mother of the Saviour and Mother of mankind, which expresses itself in genuine forms of devotion and is led to "the imitation of her virtues,"[66] above all to a decisive commitment to live according to the commandments of God and to do his will (cf. Mt 7:21; Jn 15:14);

c) develop the *capacity to communicate* such love to the Christian people through speech, writing and example, so that their Marian piety may be promoted and cultivated.

35. There are numerous advantages to be derived from an adequate Mariological formation in which the ardor of faith and the commitment to study are harmoniously composed:

— on the *intellectual level*, so that the truth about God, about Man, about Christ and about the Church are understood the more in understanding the "truth about Mary";

— on the *spiritual level*, so that such formation will help a Christian to welcome the Mother of Jesus and "bring her into everything that makes up his inner life";[67]

— on the *pastoral level*, so that the Mother of the Lord may be strongly felt as a presence of grace among the Christian people.

36. The study of Mariology holds as its ultimate aim the acquisition of a sound Marian spirituality, an essential aspect of

Christian spirituality. On his pilgrim way to the measure of the stature of the fullness of Christ (Ep 4:13), knowing the mission which God has entrusted to the Virgin in the history of salvation and in the life of the Church, the Christian takes her as "mother and teacher of the spiritual life";[68] with her and like her, in the light of the Incarnation and of Easter, he impresses on his very existence a decisive orientation towards God through Christ in the Spirit, in order to express by his life in the Church the radical message of the Good News, especially the commandment of love (cf. Jn 15:12).

Your Eminence, Your Excellencies, Reverend Rectors of Seminaries, Reverend Presidents and Deans of Ecclesiastical Faculties, we trust that these brief guidelines will be responsibly received by teachers and students and will bring forth welcome fruits.

Wishing you the abundance of God's blessings, we remain,

Yours devotedly in Our Lord,

William Cardinal Baum	Antonio M. Javierre Ortas
Prefect	*Tit. Archbishop of Meta*
	Secretary

Endnotes

[1] Synodus Episcoporum, *Ecclesiæ sub Verbo Dei mysteria Christi celebrans pro salute mundi. Relatio finalis* (Civitas Vaticana 1985), I, 2.

[2] *Ibid.*, I, 5.

[3] *Ibid.*, I, 6.

[4] Ioannes Paulus PP. II, Litt. Enc. *Redemptoris Mater* (25 Martii 1987) 48: *AAS*79 (1987), 427.

[5] Cf. *ibid.*, 1, 25.

[6] Missale Romanum, Prex Eucharistica I, *Communicantes*.

[7] *Lumen Gentium*, 65.

[8] *Ibid.*, 52.

[9] Cf. *ibid.*, 53.

[10] *Ibid.*, 56.

[11] *Sacrosanctum Concilium*, 103.

[12] *Lumen Gentium*, 53.

[13] Cf. *Concilium Toletanum XI*, 48: Denzinger-Schönmetzer, *Enchiridion Symbolorum definitionum et declarationum de rebus fidei et morum* (Barcinone 1976), 536.

[14] Cf. *Lumen Gentium*, 57, 61.

[15] *Ibid.*, 56.

[16] *Ibid.*, 61. Cf. *ibid.*, 56, 58.

[17] *Ibid.*, 58.

[18] *Ibid.*, 56.

[19] Cf. *ibid.*, 53.

[20] Cf. *ibid.*, 52, 63, 65.

[21] *Ibid*, 59.

[22] *Ibid.*, 53.

[23] Paulus PP. VI, Allocutio tertia SS. Concili periodo exacta (21 Novembris 1964): *AAS56* (1964), 1014-1018.

[24] Cf. *ibid.*, 64.

[25] Cf. *ibid,*, 53, 63, 65.

[26] Cf. *ibid.*, 65.

[27] Cf. *Lumen Gentium*, 62.

[28] Cf. *Lumen Gentium*, 68.

[29] *Sacrosanctum Concilium*, 103.

[30] *Lumen Gentium*, 68.

[31] Six International Marian Congresses, organized by the Pontificia Accademia Mariana Internazionale, held between 1967 and 1987, systematically studied manifestations of Marian piety from the 1st to the 20th centuries.

[32] Paulus PP. VI, Adh. Ap. *Marialis Cultus* (2 Februarii 1974) Intr.: *AAS66* (1974), 114.

[33] *Redemptoris Mater*, 31.

[34] Dimitrios I, *Homily given on 7th December 1987 during the celebration of Vespers at St. Mary Major* (Rome): *L'Osservatore Romano* (Eng. Ed. 21-28 Dec. 1987), p. 6.

[35] *Ibid.*, 6.

[36] The Ecumenical Directory provides guidelines for a Mariological formation which is attentive to ecumenical needs: Secretariatus ad Christianorum Unitatem Fovendam, *Spiritus Domini* (16 Aprilis 1970): *AAS62* (1970), 705-724.

[37] *Redemptoris Mater*, 46.

[38] Cf. 111 Conferencia General del Episcopado Latino-Americano (Puebla 1979), *La evangelizacion en el presente y en el futuro de America Latina* (Bogota 1979), 282.

[39] *Redemptoris Mater*, 45.

[40] *Ibid.*, 19.

[41] Title of part II of the Encyclical *Redemptoris Mater*.

[42] Title of part III of the Encyclical *Redemptoris Mater*.

[43] Cf. *Redemptoris Mater*, 45, 46.

[44] Cf. *ibid.*, 1, 25.

[45] Cf. *Lumen Gentium*, 65.

[46] *Marialis Cultus*, 25.

[47] *Redemptoris Mater*, 4; cf. *ibid.*, 19.

[48] *Ibid.*, 27.

[49] Cf. *ibid.*, 2.

[50] *Marialis Cultus*, 56.

[51] *Lumen Gentium*, 53.

[52] *Marialis Cultus*, 35.

[53] *Ibid.*, 57.

[54] *Redemptoris Mater*, 25.

[55] *Dei Verbum*, 24.

[56] cf. *ibid.*, 24; *Optatam Totius*, 16.

[57] *Dei Verbum*, 10.

[58] Cf. *ibid.*, 10.

[59] This Congregation has been pleased to note the dissertations for the licence or doctorate in theology which have treated Mariological themes. Persuaded of the importance of such studies and desiring their increase, in 1979 the Congregation instituted the 'licence or doctorate in theology with specialization in Mariology" (cf. Ioannes Paulus PP. II, Const. Ap. *Sapientia Christiana* (15 Aprilis 1979) Appendix II ad art. 64 "Ordinationum", n. 12: *AAS71* (1979), 520. Two centers offer this specialization: the Pontifical "Marianum" Faculty of Theology in Rome, and the International Marian Research Institute, University of Dayton, Ohio, U.S.A., which is linked to the "Marianum".

[60] *Marialis Cultus*, 57.

[61] Cf. *Sapientia Christiana*, 3.

[62] *Optatam Totius*, 8.

[63] Congregatio Pro Institutione Catholica, *Ratio fundamentalis institutionis sacerdotalis* (Romae 1985) 54 e.

[64] Id., *Circular letter concerning some of the more urgent aspects of spiritual formation in seminaries*, II, 4.

[65] Cf. *Codex Iuris Canonici*, can. 246, par. 3.

[66] *Lumen Gentium*, 67.

[67] *Redemptoris Mater*, 45.

[68] Cf. *Marialis Cultus*, 21; *Collectio massarum de b. Maria Virgine*, form. 32.

BIBLIOGRAPHY

Reference Works and Sources

Abbott, Walter M., S.J., ed. *The Documents of Vatican II.* New York: Guild Press, 1966.

Biblical Theology Bulletin: *Mary -Woman of the Mediterranean,* Vol. 20, 1990, 2.

Blinzler, J. *Die Brüder und Schwestern Jesu, (SBS21).* Stuttgart: Katholisches Bibelwerk, 1967.

Brown, R.E., Fitzmyer, J.A., Murphy, R.E. *The Jerome Biblical Commentary.* Englewood Cliffs, N.J.: Prentice-Hall, Inc., 1968.

Brown, R.E., Fitzmyer, J.A., Murphy, R.E. *The New Jerome Biblical Commentary.* Englewood Cliffs, N.J.: Prentice-Hall, Inc., 1990.

Brown, R.E., Donfried, K.P., Fitzmyer, J.A., Reumann, J., eds. *Mary in the New Testament: A Collaborative Assessment by Protestant and Roman Catholic Scholars.* Philadelphia: Fortress Press, 1978.

Brown, Raymond E. *The Birth of the Messiah: A Commentary on the Infancy Narratives in Matthew and Luke.* New York: Doubleday & Co., Inc., 1977.

Brown, Raymond E. *The Virginal Conception and Bodily Resurrection of Jesus.* New York: Paulist Press, 1973.

Buby, Bertrand, S.M. *Biblical Exegesis in Greek Patristic Texts* (dissertation). Dayton, OH: International Marian Research Institute, 1979.

De Fiores, S. and Meo, S. *Nuovo Dizionario di Mariologia.* Milano: Edizioni Paoline, 1986.

de la Potterie, Ignace, S.J., (Buby, Bertrand, S.M., trans.) *Mary in the Mystery of the Covenant.* Staten Island, N.Y.: Alba House, 1992.

Di Berardino, Angelo. *Encyclopedia of the Early Church,* Vols. 1 & 2. New York: Oxford University Press, 1992.

Fuller, Reginald, ed. *A New Catholic Commentary on Holy Scripture.* Nashville: Nelson, 1975.

Fitzmyer, Joseph A., S.J., comm. *The Historical Truth of the Gospels: The 1964 Instruction of the Biblical Commission.* Glen Rock, N.J.: Paulist Press, 1964.

Koehler, Theodore A., S.M., ed. *Marian Studies* Vols. 1-44 Dayton, OH: Mariological Society of America, 1950-1993.

Laurentin, René. *Structure et Théologie de Luc I-II. Etudes Bibliques.* Paris: J. Gabalda, 1957.

Machen, J. Gresham. *The Virgin Birth of Christ.* Grand Rapids: Baker Book House Co., 1960.

Metzger, Bruce M. *A Textual Commentary on the Greek New Testament.* New York: United Bible Societies, 1971.

O'Carroll, Michael, C.S.Sp. *Theotokos: A Theological Encyclopedia of the Blessed Virgin Mary.* Wilmington, Del.: Glazier-Liturgical Press, 1982.

Peake, Arthur S. *Peake's Commentary on the Bible.* London: T. Nelson, 1964.

Rossano, P., Ravasi, G., Girlanda, A. *Nuovo Dizionario di Teologia Biblica.* Milano: Edizioni Paoline, 1988.

Roten, Johann G., S.M., ed. *Mater Fidei et Fidelium, Collected Essays to Honor Theodore Koehler on His 80th Birthday.* (Marian Library Studies, Vols. 17-23, 1985-1991). Dayton, OH: University of Dayton, 1991.

Schneiders, Sandra. *The Revelatory Text.* San Francisco: Harper & Row, 1991.

Serra, Aristide, O.S.M. *E C'era la Madre di Gesù (Gv. 2,1): saggi di esegesi biblico-mariana (1978-1988).* Milano: Edizioni Cens-Marianum, 1989.

Strack, H., and Billerbeck, P. *Kommentar zum Neuen Testament aus Talmud und Midrasch* (6 Vols.). Munich: C.H. Beck, 1922-1961.

Theotokos: Ricerche Interdisciplinari. Roma: Montfortane, I, 1993/2.

Commentaries and Articles on the Gospels and St. Paul

Alfaro, Juan. "The Mariology of the Fourth Gospel." *Biblical Theology Bulletin* 10 #1 (1980), 3-16.

Anderson, H. "Broadening Horizons: The Rejection of Nazareth Pericope of Lk 4:16-30 in Light of Recent Critical Trends." *Interpretation* 18 (1964), 259-75.

Barrett, Charles Kingsley. *The Gospel According to John.* Philadelphia: Westminster, 1978.

Beare, F.W. *The Earliest Records of Jesus.* New York: Abingdon Press, 1962.

Benko, S. *The Virgin Goddess: Studies in the Pagan and Christian roots of Mariology.* Leiden and New York: E.J. Brill, 1993.

Branscomb, B.H. *Commentary on St. Mark's Gospel.* London: Hodder & Stoughton, 1952.

Brown, Raymond E. *The Gospel According to John* (The Anchor Bible, Vols. 29 & 29a). Garden City, N.Y.: Doubleday, 1966 & 1970.

Buby, Bertrand, S.M. "A Christology of Relationship in Mark." *Biblical Theology Bulletin* 10 (Oct. 1980), 149-54.

Buby, Bertrand, S.M. "Mary, A Model of Ecclesia-Orans in Acts 1:14." *Marian Studies* 35 (1984), 87-99.

Buby, Bertrand, S.M. "The Biblical Prayer of Mary." *Review for Religious* 39 (1980), 577-581.

Buby, Bertrand, S.M. "The Commitment of Faith and Love in the Fourth Gospel." *Review for Religious* 40 #4 (1981), 561-567.

Bultmann, Rudolf. *The Gospel of John*. Philadelphia: Westminster, 1971.

Cadbury, H.J. *The Making of Luke-Acts*. New York: Macmillan, 1927.

Crosby, M. *House of Disciples: Church, Economics, and Justice in Matthew*. New York: Orbis Books, 1988.

de Goedt, M. "Un Schème de Révélation dans le quatrième Evangile." *New Testament Studies* 8 (1961-62), 142-150.

de la Potterie, Ignace, S.J. *The Hour of Jesus: The Passion and the Resurrection of Jesus According to John*. Staten Island, NY: Alba House, 1989.

Deiss, Lucien. *Mary Daughter of Sion*. Collegeville, MN: Liturgical Press, 1972.

Dillon, Richard. "Wisdom Tradition and Sacramental Retrospect in the Cana Account (Jn 2,1-11)." *Catholic Biblical Quarterly* 24 (1962), 268-96.

Ellis, Peter. *The Genius of John: A Composition-Critical Commentary on the Fourth Gospel*. Collegeville: Liturgical Press, 1984.

Feuillet, André. *Jesus and His Mother*. Still River, Mass.: Bede, 1984.

Feuillet, André. *Johannine Studies*. Staten Island, NY: Alba House, 1965.

Fitzmyer, Joseph A., S.J. *The Gospel According to Luke* (The Anchor Bible, Vols. 28 and 28a). Garden City, N.Y.: Doubleday, 1981, 1985.

Fitzmyer, Joseph A., S.J. *Luke the Theologian*. New York: Paulist Press, 1989.

Fortna, R.T. *The Gospel of Signs*. Cambridge, UK: Cambridge University Press, 1970.

Garafalo, Robert. *History, Theology and Symbol: The Mother of Jesus in the Cana Narrative, 1950-1990* (unpublished thesis). Dayton, OH: International Marian Research Institute, 1993.

Girard, Marc. "La composition structurelle des sept signes dans le quatrième evangile." *Studies in Religion/Science Religieuse* 9 #3 (1980), 315-324.

Grassi, Joseph, "The Role of Jesus' Mother in John's Gospel: A Re-appraisal." *Catholic Biblical Quarterly* 48 (1986), 67-90.

Grassi, Joseph. "The Wedding at Cana (John II:1-11): A Pentecostal Meditation?" *Novum Testamentum* 14 (1972), 131-36.

Hill, D. "The Rejection of Jesus at Nazareth (Luke IV:16-30)." *Novum Testamentum* 13 (1971), 161-80.

Hofrichter, P. *Nicht aus Blut Sondern monogen aus Gott Geboren. Textkritische Untersuchung zu Joh 1, 13-14*. Würzburg, 1978.

Hoskyns, Edward. *The Fourth Gospel*. London: Faber and Faber, 1947.

Johnson, M.D. *The Purpose of the Biblical Genealogies with Special Reference to the Setting of the Genealogies of Jesus*. (New Testament Studies monograph series #8). Cambridge University Press, 1969.

Keck, L. and Martyn, J.L., eds. *Studies in Luke-Acts*. Nashville/New York: Abingdon Press, 1966.

Kingsbury, Jack D. *Matthew: Structure, Christology, Kingdom*. Philadelphia: Fortress Press, 1975.

190 *Mary of Galilee: Volume I*

Koehler, Theodore, S.M. "Les principales interprétations de Jn. 19,25-27, pendant les douzes premiers siècles." *Etudes Mariales* 16 (1959), 119-155.

Lathrop, G.W. *Who Shall Describe His Origin?: Tradition and Redaction in Mark 6:1-6a* (dissertation). Nijmegan, 1969.

Laurentin, René. (Wrenn, M.J., trans.). *The Truth of Christmas Beyond the Myths: the Gospels of the Infancy of Christ.* Petersham, Massachusetts: Bede, 1986.

Lindars, B. *The Gospel of John.* London: Oliphants, 1972.

Mac Rae, George, S.J. *Invitation to John.* Garden City, N.Y.: Image Books, 1978.

Maddox, R. (Rickes, J., ed.). *The Purpose of Luke-Acts.* Edinburgh: T & T Clark, 1982.

Maynard, A.H. "Ti emoi kai soi [Greek idiom; Jn 2:4]." *New Testament Studies* 31 (1985), 582-86.

McHugh, J. *The Mother of Jesus in the New Testament.* London: Darton, 1975.

Meier, J.P. "The Brothers and Sisters of Jesus in Ecumenical Perspective." *Catholic Biblical Quarterly* 54 (1992), 1-28.

Moloney, F.J. *Belief in the Word: Reading John 1-4.* Minneapolis: Fortress Press, 1993.

Moloney, F. J. "From Cana to Cana (John 2:1-4:54) and the Fourth Evangelist's Concept of Correct (and Incorrect) Faith." *Salesianum* 40 (1978), 817-843. (Also in *Studia Biblica* 1978).

Moloney, F.J. *Mary: Woman and Mother.* Homebush: St. Paul Publications, 1988.

Moloney, F.J. "Mary in the Fourth Gospel: Woman and Mother." *Salesianum* 51 (1989), 421-40.

Montefiore, C.G. *The Synoptic Gospels Vol. I* (2nd edition). London: Macmillan, 1927.

Nelson, R.D. "David: A Model for Mary in Luke?" *Biblical Theology Bulletin* 18 (1988), 138-142.

Nolan, Mary Catherine, O.P. *Mary's Song: Canticle of a Liberated People* (unpublished thesis). Dayton, OH: International Marian Research Institute, 1992.

Perrin, Norman. *Rediscover ng the Teachings of Jesus.* New York: Harper & Row, 1967.

Plummer, A. *St. Luke. The International Critical Commentary.* Edinburgh: Clark, 1981.

Ratzinger, Joseph. *Daughter Zion.* San Francisco: Ignatius 1983.

Schillebeeckx, E. and Halkes, C. *Mary: Yesterday - Today - Tomorrow.* New York: Crossroad, 1993.

Schnackenburg, R. *The Gospel According to John* (3 vols). New York: Crossroad, 1968-1982.

Sloyan, G. *John: Interpretation.* Atlanta: Knox, 1988.

Talbert, C.H., ed. *Literary Patterns, Theological Themes and the Genre of Luke-Acts.* Missoula: Scholars Press, 1974.

Talbert, C.H., ed. *Perspectives on Luke-Acts.* (multiple contributors) Danville, VA: Association of Baptist Professors of Religion, 1978.

Talbert, C.H., ed. *Luke-Acts: New Perspectives from the Society of Biblical Literature Seminar.* New York: Crossroad, 1984.

Talbert, C.H. *Reading Luke - A Literary and Theological Commentary on the Third Gospel.* New York: Crossroad, 1982.

Taylor, V. *The Gospel According to St Mark.* New York: Macmillan, 1966.

Vanhoye, Albert, S.J. "Interrogation et exégèse de Cana (Jn 2,4)." *Biblica* 55 (1974), 157-167.

Vanhoye, Albert, S.J. "La Mère du Fils de Dieu selon Ga 4,4." *Marianum* 40 (1978), 237-47.

Wainwright, Elaine Mary. *Towards a Feminist Critical Reading of the Gospel According to Matthew.* New York: De Gruyter, 1991.

Other Literature or Media

Bearsley, P. "Mary the Perfect Disciple: A Paradigm for Mariology." *Theological Studies* 41 (1980), 461-504.

Bossman, D.M., ed. "Mary - Woman of the Mediterranean." (Special Issue). *Biblical Theology Bulletin* 20 #2, 1990.

Brennan, Walter, O.S.M. *Mary: Servant, Mother, Woman.* Chicago: Friar Servants of Mary, 1986.

Brennan, Walter, O.S.M. *The Sacred Memory of Mary.* New York: Paulist Press, 1988.

Brown, Raymond E. *Biblical Exegesis and Church Doctrine.* New York: Paulist Press, 1985.

Carroll, Eamon R., O. Carm. *Understanding the Mother of Jesus.* Wilmington, Del.: Glazier, 1979.

Corsini, Eugenio (Moloney, F.J., S.D.B., trans.). *The Apocalypse: The Perennial Revelation of Jesus Christ.* Wilmington, Del: Michael Glazier, 1983.

Donnelly, D., ed. *Mary: Woman of Nazareth: Biblical and Theological Perspectives.* New York: Paulist Press, 1989.

Dyer, George, ed. "Miryam, Woman of Nazareth." (Dedicated issue, multiple contributors). *Chicago Studies* 27 #1 (1988), 3-108.

Ford, J. Massyngberde, *Revelation.* (The Anchor Bible, Vol. 38). Garden City, N.Y.: Doubleday & Company, Inc., 1975.

Jelly, Frederick M., O.P. *Madonna: Mary in the Catholic Tradition.* Huntington, Indiana: Our Sunday Visitor, 1986.

Johnson, Elizabeth A. *She Who Is: The Mystery of God in Feminist Theological Discourse.* New York: Crossroad, 1992.

Laurentin, René. *A Short Treatise on the Blessed Virgin Mary.* Washington, New Jersey: AMI Press, 1991.

Macquarrie, J. *Mary for All Christians*. Grand Rapids: Eerdmans, 1990.

National Conference of Catholic Bishops. *Behold Your Mother*. Washington, D.C.: USCC, 1973.

Nunzio, Lemmo. "Maria, 'Figlia di Sion', a partire da Lc 1, 26-28, Bilancio esegetico dal 1939 al 1982." (doctoral dissertation). *Marianum* 45 (1983), 175- 258.

Pelikan, J., Flusser, D., and Lang, J. *Mary: Images of the Mother of Jesus in Jewish and Christian Perspective*. Philadelphia: Fortress Press, 1986.

Pope John Paul II. *Mother of the Redeemer*. Boston: Daughters of Saint Paul, 1987.

Prévost, J. P. *Mother of Jesus*. Ottowa: Novalis, 1988.

Roten, Johann, S.M., ed. *Mary in Faith and Life in the New Age of the Church*. Dayton, OH: International Marian Research Institute, 1983.

Schaberg, Jane. *The Illegitimacy of Jesus: A Feminist Theological Interpretation of the Infancy Narratives*. San Francisco: Harper & Row, 1987.

Tambasco, A. *What Are They Saying About Mary?* New York: Paulist Press, 1984.

Wohlmann, Avital. "Mary of Nazareth: Why the Silence of Judaism?" *SIDIC* 20 #2 (1987), 9-14.

Zukowski, Angela Ann, M.H.S.H., ed. *Vatican II Vision 2000, Part 5 of 6: Mary: Model of Contemporary Discipleship*. (Videotape, May 28, 1991). Dayton, OH 45469-0314: University of Dayton Center for Religious Telecommunications, 1991.